Y

YOUNG MAN, YOU'LL NEVER DIE

YOUNG MAN, YOU'LL NEVER DIE

Merton Naydler

ISIS
LARGE PRINT
Oxford

First published in Great Britain 2005
by Pen & Sword Aviation
an imprint of
Pen & Sword Books Ltd.

Published in Large Print 2006 by ISIS Publishing Ltd.,
7 Centremead, Osney Mead, Oxford OX2 0ES
by arrangement with
Pen & Sword Books Ltd.

British Library Cataloguing in Publication Data
Naydler, Merton
    Young man, you'll never die. – New ed., Large print ed.
    (Isis reminiscence series)
    1. Naydler, Merton 2. Great Britain. Royal Air
    Force – History – World War, 1939–1945
    3. Fighter pilots – Great Britain – Biography
    4. World War, 1939–1945 – Aerial operations, British
    5. World War, 1939–1945 – Personal narratives, British
    6. World War, 1939–1945 – Campaigns – Burma
    7. World War, 1939–1945 – Campaigns – Africa, North
    8. Large type books
    I. Title
    940.5'44'941'092

ISBN–10 0–7531–9388–4 (hb)
ISBN–13 978–0–7531–9388–4

ISBN 978–0–7531–9389–1 (pb)

Printed and bound in Great Britain by
T. J. International Ltd., Padstow, Cornwall

TO THE YOUNG MEN WHO DID

Contents

Although this story is the experience of one man, with slight variations it represents that of many. And after a lifetime of sublimation it can be told without fear of being shot down in flames — the "dreaded fate" of the "line-shooter" of old.

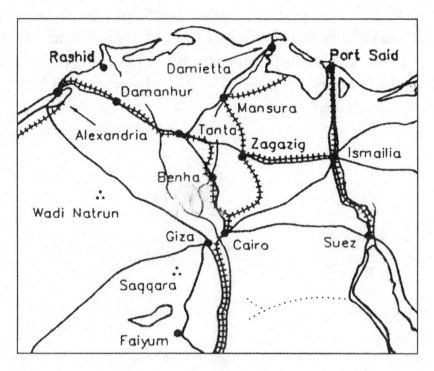

Northern Egypt, showing location of Wadi Natrun

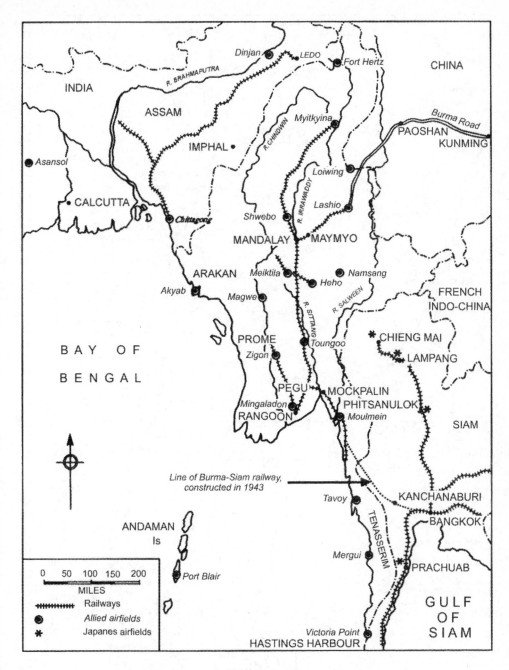

Map of India and Burma

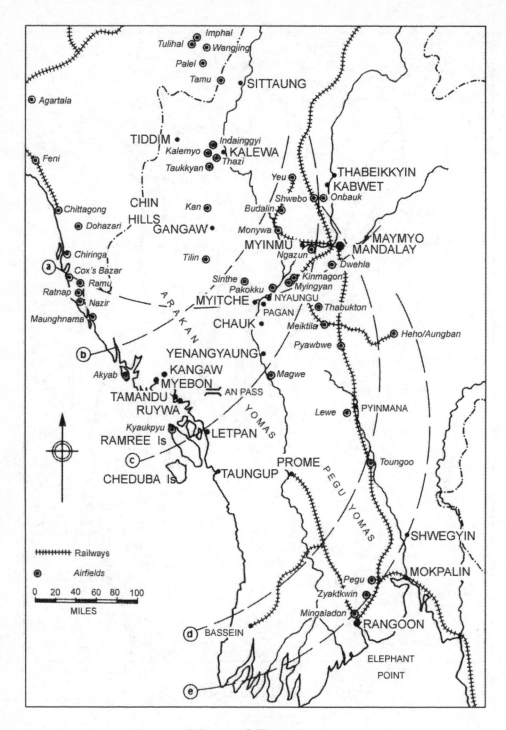

Map of Burma

CHAPTER
ONE

Initiation

"'Ere," said the squad Sergeant in confiding tones to the fifty rookies standing easy on the draughty seafront — "'ad a smashing bird last night." Across the pavement behind where he stood facing us, the thin boarding-houses where we were billeted blinked in the weak March sun. We were a captive audience, in his eyes another pretty hopeless bunch of recruits; he himself was not a "regular" airman but an extremely fit (physically) East End heavyweight boxing pro with a suitably broken nose and cauliflower ears, very appropriate to lick us into some sort of necessary physical shape. He was well over six feet tall, four or more feet across the shoulders, and tapered steadily through slim hips to slender ankles — kite-shaped. The otherwise boring foot-drill, executed uncertainly under the rheumy appraisal of retired local inhabitants, was relieved by his generous intimacies.

"Cor stone me bloomin' 'ooray! Three-quarters of an hour I kept it up last night . . ." The recruits, nineteen or twenty years old, were learning about Life as well as foot-drill, and about Death too, by way of the unpleasant business of blood-letting with rifle and bayonet. It took some time to recover from the inferiority induced by the Sergeant's amatory revelations.

"Cor stone the bleedin' crows," he reminisced, justifiably.

Help was at hand in the guise of a kind lady whose husband was away in the Navy; I resembled him sufficiently to enable her to become confused about which of us I was. Fortunately, the Air Force had by now stopped putting bromide in our tea, relying instead on subduing our libidos by an assortment of daily inoculations and vaccinations. Nevertheless, frequent anatomical examination established our continuing freedom from love's infections, and only occasionally was a shamefaced airman edged off to the prophylactic clinic.

As a very young man I was more a poet than man of action, vague and woolly, preoccupied with writing indifferent rhymes and songs, roused only by injustice or physical violence. At that stage I could not reasonably anticipate the circumstances which were to cast me to distant places, the often ridiculous way of life which was to become everyday, the men who in their hundreds would share my journey part way, only to fall victim to their own personalities or the perils of wartime flying, or both. Nor, in the enormous buoyancy of youth could I foresee the agonies which ineptitude was to occasion, nor how experience was to outwit incapacity, and confidence supplant fear. I was to see many die, and not a few would I kill, though at no time — least of all when it was happening — did I address my mind in a direct way to the fact that I would be or actually was destroying life — not in the bloodlust of hand-to-hand battle, but remotely and impersonally from the skies, a bit like God Himself.

In the flush of youthful enthusiasm then in the first stages of supplanting my natural fear, thus dislike, of violence, I had no inkling of the harsher crust which was to encase the softness of adolescence and eliminate much of the idyllic dreamer, or of the cynical bitterness which was to grow alongside slow realisation of futility, and of the opportunism of those to whom war was just another fiddle in an ongoing career of opportunism and fiddling. With little idea of what I was heading for, without a trace of hero in my make-up, I could least of all envision the successive years of war which as a callow youth I was blindly entering, and throughout which an almost magical charm was to preserve me when, over and over again, my life should have been lost, or at least my young body broken. I was at the threshhold of a strange career which was to absorb the first five long years of my adult life.

On Sunday September 3rd 1939 I was playing tennis and eighteen years of age, and had goggled at the balloon barrage hoisted over Manchester and Salford two days earlier when Hitler and Stalin invaded Poland from opposite ends. For at least the three previous years my generation had been in no doubt that we were in for it, and had indulged in self-conscious jokes about the itchiness of khaki uniforms. When I was seventeen, a fairground gipsy who understood about international politics had told me my lifeline ended abruptly at the age of twenty-five. The way we youngsters then felt about the prophesy, that impending conflict, seemed no smarter than forecasting the prospects of a man about to face a firing squad; but twenty-five was a long way ahead. We did not question the circumstances which were to affect our lives so profoundly, did not blame anybody, just mutely accepted the natural forces which nobody could control. Those men a couple of years older than us had been conscripted into the Armed Forces or the coalmines and disliked both, though for many from our industrially depressed area it was a notable improvement on just hanging around the murky street-corners asking the inevitable question: "Are you workin', kid?"

I listened matter-of-factly to Mr Chamberlain's bleated announcement on the radio that a state of war existed between us and Germany. What else could one expect? — at least his appeasement had given us an extra year to get ready.

The ensuing month I was to start a University course, but this turned out to be a first-class farce, thanks to me rather than the Führer. While France was crumbling in Spring 1940 I was supposedly engrossed in my books, but had so little stomach for learning that my presence within Academe's cloisters ceased to be relevant. June 1940 saw the remnants of the British Expeditionary Force, ill-fated debris of Dunkirk, lying exhausted on our suburban pavements. At about the same time France fell, and refused the offer of Union from our new Prime Minister, Winston Churchill. I was briskly keen to obey his stirring injunction to confront the expected invader with pitchfork or pike, for he had managed to inspire a mood in which at least the young warriors of our society were keen and willing to fight to the death, barehanded if need be — an aspect of insanity which I was to encounter in a far distant foe, as yet unthought-of.

When the lull which lasted until September 1940 came to an end with the Battle of Britain I felt a sense of shame that I was not taking part. My attention was drawn to the realities of the situation when, at the unexpected hour of two in the afternoon, a pencil-slim Dornier 17 absent-mindedly dropped a bomb across the square outside Harrogate Railway Station, where I was en route to my first love. A day or two later, as we walked together up a lane on the edge of York, a bored German pilot released his load into a field just ahead of us. I heard the bombs whistle ever more loudly as they plummeted, but didn't realise what they were until they hit the ground and exploded, the sudden shock jumping me clean off both feet into the quivering air. We giggled at each other's fright, then exchanged a kiss of relief.

The Battle of Britain was hardly over before successive raids flattened Manchester's centre, my knees literally knocking at each great wallop. The mobile anti-aircraft guns which seemed to go off repeatedly outside our front door reverberated a deafening thunder-roll, hollowly through the interminable night. The wail of air-raid sirens became customary. Incendiary bombs rained down from the black sky to burn in our back garden, our attic, our front garden, and the house opposite which was ablaze, while we wielded our stirrup pump to extinguish the fire in the attic; every house had a stirrup pump. The centre of the town was an inferno, and next morning I gawked at the litter of smashed buildings, and roads littered with rubble and glass fragments and hosepipes, with water running everywhere. I sheltered from the destruction in our cellar, in bomb-shelters below the cathedral, even in shop doorways, from which I watched anti-aircraft cannon send up spectacular strings of lethal coloured bubbles, flinching as lacerating shrapnel lumps clattered down into the streets and on to the roofs. Lurid skies, leaping with flame and smoke, taught us what hell looks like. I darted from the cover of one doorway to the next, making a fearful way home to what damage awaited me.

In November 1940, before my twentieth birthday, I enlisted in the Royal Air Force as an aircraftsman second-class, to be trained as a pilot, and was sent back home with a piece of paper identifying me as "1233912 AC2 Naydler, M. U/T (Under Training) Pilot/Observer/Air-gunner." Impatiently I awaited orders to report for duty. "We'll send for you," they had told me. Meanwhile the night bombing continued, the railway stations were wrecked, hundreds died, and still I awaited the summons to arms. An oil bomb demolished the house in which I was sheltering with friends, leaving us lying in several inches of suffocating soot under an open night sky, red and frightening with flames and stifling with the stench of oil smoke. Shocked, I almost wept at the gallantry of the volunteer Street Wardens, there among the debris of the house almost before I was back on my feet. When my parents' house was hit a second time they sensibly cleared off to the Fylde coast for safety, while I lodged with my sister near the docks and munitions factories at Old Trafford. Her husband was a doctor, and both of them were in the thick of it where they lived, while I mooned around, waiting.

Like many of my generation, I had brought myself up on books about World War I. Particularly, I cherished a blue-bound book of war stories on the cover of which a black line drawing showed two Tommies back to back with heads bowed, rifles with attached bayonets held slackly with butts on the ground, between them a Union Jack; to me they were paying homage to a million dead comrades. The qualities of courage and heroism within the book were quite alien to my excessively gentle nature. But the stories which really enthralled me were those about Sopwith Pups and Camels, SE5s, Fokker tri-planes, Hell's Angels, Bishop, Ball, Richthofen's Circus, Baldy's Angels every week in the tuppenny bloods — marvellous heroic stuff whose intoxication seeped deep into my boy's soul. Equally I was alive to the drab mockery of the Armistice Days celebrated every November 11th throughout my boyhood, and whose effeteness became increasingly obvious as 1936 succeeded 1935, and so on through to the outbreak of the Second World War less than twenty-one years after the first Armistice Day. From the age of fifteen I refused to participate in the idiotic travesty and stood my two minutes' silence in flushed mutiny. "O God, our help in ages past," they sang, and then "Be Thou our guard whilst troubles last," which sounded almost flirtatious. Anyway, should God really be "Thou"? What had become known as the War to End Wars obviously hadn't worked and we boys knew it to have been a bloody shambles of squandered lives and opportunity. We knew too that we would be the uncomplaining fodder of the next one.

But my boyhood reading left little else to be considered. The elderly politicians had always got it right. Throughout history they had always known how to manipulate the young warriors, and for all my timidity I was no exception. Corpuscle-wise I was brimming with fighterdom, strafing, Very pistols, dawn reconaissances, patrols and dogfights, and I was excitedly aware of the Hun in the sun. The romantic notions pushed aside the poet-composer as my thoughts flew to the day when I would sport a large moustache and display a pilot's wings badge on the left breast of a Royal Air Force uniform.

March 1941 at last brought orders to report to RAF Station, Cardington, collecting a party of four other recruits en route at Preston railway station. Like countless practical mothers since the beginning of time, mine blinked away her tears and showed me how to sow and darn, which turned out to be useful knowledge. The railway station at Preston became the setting for my first war contribution, as I assembled my charges. A few hours later I presented them and myself in good order, with the suitcases we had brought with us for sending home our civilian clothes; things were taking a sombre turn.

The first happening was an interview before a Board of four dignified gentlemen in Air Force uniforms with lots of braid stitched on; it went along these lines:

THEM:	Why do you want to fly?
ME:	I've always been interested in flying and I think I have the right qualifications.
THEM:	Ever fired a gun?
ME:	Well . . . no. (Should I tell them I hated loud bangs?)
THEM:	Not a rifle?
ME:	No.
THEM:	(hopefully) OTC? (which in those days meant Officers Training Corps, not Over the Counter).
ME:	There wasn't one at our school.
THEM:	An airgun, then?
ME:	'Fraid not.
THEM:	(becoming exasperated) Surely an air pistol!
ME:	No. (Pause for whispered confabulation by Board).
THEM:	(very pointedly) Are you quite sure?

I began to understand that it mattered to them. I reflected on the potato-guns and water-pistols of a few

9

years earlier when I was still in short trousers, but thought that wouldn't go down too well.

ME: Well, I once fired a friend's pistol.

A sigh of relief. It was true — a friend whose name I couldn't remember had a sort of toy air pistol at least seven years earlier when I was twelve, and I had had one nervous go at it. I remembered because he had hit another boy in the leg with a pellet and we both had to run for it, even though I was innocent. That seemed to satisfy them and they said they'd put me down to train as aircrew. I asked what that meant and they said Pilot or Navigator or Air-gunner, like my bit of paper had said. No, I said, I didn't want to be an air-gunner. (I'd heard too many bloody stories about what happened to Tail-end Charlies, and in any case I preferred to see where I was going rather than where I'd been.) Nor did I want to be a navigator. It was a pilot I wanted to be. They were sorry, they said politely yet firmly, but there wasn't any choice. Pilot or navigator or air-gunner I'd be up in the air. I said I too was sorry, but in that case I might as well be a soldier. After some debate they realised that I was still a civilian, and that seemed to floor them. Grumpily they crossed out navigator and air-gunner. My career as a barrack-room lawyer had begun.

I was submitted to stringent medical tests applied to expectant aircrew and felt thoroughly ill at the twirlings-around and lung-extending, dizzy-making blood-pressure ordeals to which I was subjected before being pronounced A1, and required to be comforted by the assurance that it was nothing like that when you were actually flying. In those days you were A1 if you were warm.

I was duly sworn in and given or not given the King's penny or shilling (at all events there was talk about it), received my airman's uniform, and went home with my suitcase of civilian clothes to bid goodbye to family and friends, ill-dressed in Air Force blue with brass buttons, and lumpy large black pimply boots which never stopped hurting my soft ankles. I had never felt more self-conscious.

A few days later I was back at Cardington, housed in a timber hut with a couple of dozen fellow-recruits and drinking regular cups of tea (that's where they put in the bromide), avoiding peeling bucketsful of potatoes except when conscripted by the corporal — "I want three volunteers: you, you and you!" — evading also the cleaning out of latrines and having the hair cropped, and being awakened at half-past six by the savage bellow of the corporal in charge of our hut, who slept in a separate bit at one end.

"Wakey WAKEY!" he roared — "Rise and shine, morning's fine, show a leg, come along there — S T I R ! ! ! you lazy swine!"

In no time nought became zero and teatime sixteen-fifteen hours, then we went, a thousand strong, to learn an airman's basic disciplines at Skegness — marching up and down the promenade, turning and wheeling, the use of rifle and bayonet, and various exclusively RAF expressions.

Late for my supper one evening I was told by the sergeant who was head cook that I had had it. I stood there with my mess tin and irons, the name given to knife, fork and spoon. "No, sergeant," I explained to him patiently, "I haven't. You see?" showing him my unused implements.

"You bloody 'ave, mate," he insisted.

"Honestly, sergeant, I haven't!" My voice was only slightly raised, as I was confused more than cross.

"You may not think you 'ave, but you fucking 'ave!"

I faced him in blank incomprehension. I knew I hadn't had my supper, I'd shown him the evidence, and here he was insisting that I had. I didn't know what to say next. There was an obvious breakdown in communications. He seemed to read my perplexity.

"Look, mate," he said in a kindlier tone, "we finish dishing up at 19.30 hours. You've 'ad yours. Better be on time in future."

Sad and empty, but with important new intelligence, I departed.

And I learnt other things — a special kind of whistle to indicate approbation of the turns at the local music-hall which we visited weekly, the delight of fried eggs and chips, a wide repertoire of everyday swear words, and some impressive blasphemies for special occasions. I earned my first punishment after absenting myself without leave one idle weekend to visit a lady love. So humble was my station that I never dreamt my thirty-six hour absence would be noted, but it was, and I was suitably shaken to be placed under arrest upon my return. They'd even sent a policeman to my parents' house in case I'd deserted. Didn't they know I was going to be a pilot! With an airman on either side of me I was marched hatless in front of a charming Group Captain who lectured me on the perils of indiscipline before sentencing me to Eleven Days Confined To Barracks, which meant that instead of being free to eat egg and chips in the evenings and canoodle with the Navy gentleman's wife I had instead to sweep and scrub office floors. In fact, I simply got in the way of the ladies professionally employed for the purpose, and to keep me tidy they made me innumerable cups of tea and gave me magazines to read.

At the end of three months we were marching and drilling like professionals, we could do all the finer bits of what we called "One Pause Two", parade techniques such as are seen at Royal Tournaments and Tattoos, we had bruised shoulders from firing the heavy .303 service rifles despite padding our uniforms with the blue woollen RAF gloves, and we had charged yelling to stick our bayonets into straw dummies hanging on lines on the beach, twisting as they were withdrawn (in order to remove the intestines), before reversing our rifles and clouting under imaginary chins with the butt end. But in case that was insufficient, we then stabbed down into pretend prostrate bodies, and then placed a boot on them to facilitate withdrawal of our weapons. I don't believe any of us much enjoyed any of it, but soon enough it became time to join a class of fifty at the Aircrew Initial Training Wing at Leuchars, a huge RAF station near Dundee. In three months there we were taught the theory of everything one needed to know about aeroplanes and flying. Known as "U/T Aircrew" ("U/T" meant "Under Training") we were distinguished from the other airmen by white flashes stuck in the front of our forage caps. But we also had to keep up our drilling, and were now placed under the merciless charge of a World War I Army sergeant with a fierce waxed moustache with lethal points, who made us perform at alarming speeds on the parade-ground.

I contrived my first flight, as passenger in the back of an Anson patrolling the skies off Leuchars, and when we got back to terra firma I had to mop up the mess I had made all over the floor of their fuselage. My reaction to the plane's gentle manoeuvres bode ill for my future flying career.

Early on one of those summer mornings, the curious spluttering of unfamiliar aero-engines eased me out of bed to witness a large, strange four-engined plane approach to make a landing. With a few keen companions I raced to the airfield to investigate a Russian TB-7 bomber. Our enthusiasm diminished when we were uncompromisingly warned away by the Soviet comrades standing guard with sub-machine guns pointed at us. Grinning in what was intended to be a disarming manner I made a crisp approach to a squat ugly fellow in dark green uniform, who growled slushy words of warning and wiggled his gun. Patiently I persisted with clear and unambiguous signs that I too was a flier (had I not undergone the nauseous Anson trip) and before long we were chatting animatedly in international sign-language. They had left Moscow six hours earlier and their passenger was Molotov, then Foreign Minister and to become famous for the petrol bomb named after him. Arm in arm, the slushy one and I embarked into the bleak belly of the bare metal monster, its dark green painted interior relieved only by great mounds of beautiful furs which had kept the important passenger warm. Half a dozen of the Russians lodged at Leuchars awaiting their master's return from a London conference, and to express the enormous admiration we felt for their handling of the Germans at the time, in our youthful exuberance we took to giving them exaggerated salutes whenever our paths crossed.

Those of us who had successfully lasted the Initial Training Wing course moved on to an Aircrew Receiving Centre at Regents Park, London NW1, to await posting to an Elementary Flying Training School. There in the great metropolis I learnt to polish my service boots, for during our two weeks' stay there was little else to do besides collecting our flying kit, at Lord's cricket ground — quantities of quilted inner-suits, waterproof outer-suits with large pockets in the knees for carrying maps, heaven knows how many pairs of gloves — silk inners, woollen middles and leather gauntlet outers — fur-lined zip-fronted suede flying-boots, and a splendid leather flying-helmet complete with large goggles and earphones which fixed inside pockets tailored in the vicinity of the ears. Boots were polished by first burning them to dry out the leather, boning them with an animal bone to grease them, then by applying spit and polish alternately and rubbing like mad. Some men obtained a brilliant gloss, though my boots remained utterly recalcitrant, just the same as my obdurate shoes throughout my life.

We were billeted in once-resplendent but now-commandeered blocks of flats in St John's Wood, which had been stripped to the bone before they allowed us in. It was rumoured that people had paid £8 a week for those flats — double a handsome living wage for a whole family where I came from. London was some place. We slept on the floor, on straw-filled palliasses, eight of us to a room. We weren't allowed the lifts, and seven flights of stairs was no laughing matter, especially when accoutred with half a hundredweight of equipment, such as kitbags, haversacks, rucksacks, tin helmet, mess tin and irons, all of which we were encouraged to cart around on route marches, tottering along like horses for four, five or six aimless miles there and back to and from nowhere. We fed at Regents Park Zoo on what suspiciously resembled the rejects of the other breeds, but had to wait longer than they for the revolting lumpy gobbets of greasy swill, our queues stretching well over a mile. Always hungry and short of cash (our pay was Twelve shillings and Sixpence a week), we were too well disciplined to protest, but before long took to slipping quietly away (an old soldiers' operation known as "sloping off") and bussing to Camden Town where sometimes there was egg and chips in a steamy café or, failing that, soya-bean sausages, a staple item of wartime diet. Although there were now fewer air raids, the Tube stations were nightly choked with people seeking shelter. Understandably there was a good deal of concern with skin integrity, though that didn't apply to one of my more personable room-mates, a small tough Geordie who at twenty-one had already worked down the mines long enough to have acquired the blue facial pitting of embedded coal grit and who was quite certain he was going to become an ace bomber pilot. I'm sure he did well, if he survived, though at that stage nobody thought of dying, not even of the other man dying. We were much too young and the whole thing was a bit of a giggle.

We underwent a night vision acuity test, wearing dark glasses in a black room, holding a pad marked out with raised lines and a pencil. We waited for something to happen. After a few minutes I became aware of a dim light in front of me, a slit about a foot long and a couple of inches high. "Write down what you see," we were told, and I duly told them I saw a long horizontal oblong slit of light. The light went out and reappeared, and again we had to write down what we saw. Again I told them about the long horizontal oblong slit of light, but when it appeared for a third time I began to think that they'd got it wrong and had lost their triangular, square and circular slits of light. By the fifth time my suspicions were roused. Removing the dark glasses which I'd forgotten to take off once our eyes had been supposed to become used to the dark room, I could see a vague shape on the screen, which was the slit of light. As my eyes started to come into focus the test ended and the lights were switched on and we were shown out. A hum of animated conversation buzzed around.

"Did you make the third one a County class cruiser or one of those new destroyers?" "Was the fifth a Spitfire or a Messerschmitt 109?" It was a depressing moment, but generously they rated my night vision as "poor" — there was no room for failures.

At Piccadilly Circus one evening I found myself in semi-alcoholic conversation with an enormous Scots soldier in a kilt. It was only after several minutes that I realised he was suggesting that sex with another man could be at least as interesting as with a woman, and I beat a hasty and alarmed retreat. Although the ensuing years were to be predominantly womanless, I experienced only two other encounters of that nature — despite the unnatural living conditions we were to encounter, it could not be contended that a wartime service career involved an undue amount of corruptive exposure.

I met a girl who was a communist and actually believed in free love, which was something I had heard about. London was really some place. I dismissed from my mind the creeping thoughts of a less pleasant future.

CHAPTER
TWO

Inculcation

A batch of fifty of us, the standard number for our courses, was sent to Fairoaks, an Elementary Flying School in a luxuriant quarter of Surrey where life occurred at a plushly different level from anything known in the hardy, impoverished North. Even the billets and food were superior and refined, and it dawned on me that I was on the fringe of membership of a privileged class. I found the change unobjectionable, most importantly when we were allowed to discard the crippling pimply service boots in which we had executed our One-pause-Two, and escalated to shoes. There I saw my first man die and for the first time came close to being killed myself.

I started to grow as large a moustache as I could muster, but because it was flaxen it hardly showed, even though it became quite sizeable. I never trimmed it except at its bottom edge, just above the line of the upper lip, and then only when it began to interfere with eating, and after vigorous upwards and outwards combing to give it a thick and elongated appearance. The moustache was almost de rigueur for a potential fighter-boy, although I grew mine long before I knew whether I would qualify as a pilot, let alone before my future on bombers or fighters could be deliberated. That was a typical bit of prematurity, perhaps subconsciously designed to influence those undecided events. My thoughts dwelt constantly on the day when I would leave undone the top brass button of my pear-shaped tunic and stitch red silk into the crown of my wings badge, tokens of fighter-pilotship. Those insignia of dashing manliness were widely coveted by what was described as the cream of the nation, and equally approbated by the curds and whey. It was part of an important display of confidence, good for morale.

The Fairoaks curriculum was based on flying in the morning and schooling in the afternoon, then the other way round, alternate days. In the classroom, air navigation, gunnery, meteorology, aircraft recognition and elementary engineering were pumped into us, and at last we were relieved of the seemingly pointless infantry drill by now known as square-bashing. Despite the staunch attempt by a competent and well-mannered set of instructors to hammer home information, I was an indifferent scholar, still more the dreamy poet than the practical man of action.

We learnt to fly Tiger Moths, with whom my first acquaintance remains piquantly exciting. The smell of that first Tiger down at the edge of the grass airfield — a mix of oil, petrol and dope (the special cellulose paint on the fabric surfaces), rubber, metal and leather, bakelite and body — is salivatory and unforgettable. It was also frightening. Every pilot knows the very distinctive and special aeroplane smell which entrenches itself into the odorific memory. We became acquainted with mysterious creatures called gremlins, invisible denizens of every engine, every airframe, every piece of equipment used by the RAF, their principal characteristic being mischievousness, and although in time a certain diabolical quality became identifiable, that was never referred to for fear of some sinister revenge. Gremlins were best kept on the right side of.

I flew solo after ten hours' instruction, about the average, relishing on each trip the same delight as the first time I left the ground to enter into a new element, the engine noise then the rush of air into the open cockpit, the sensation of bumping along the ground, which diminshed as momentum was gained, then the smooth gentle ascent into another dimension. But whilst deriving considerable excited pleasure from the joy of being in the air and simple aerobatics, in which one learnt to loop the loop and stall turn, I disliked intensely spinning exercises, when the plane was induced to dive vertically at a wildly rotating earth, and was clumsy at the slow roll, which was disorientating. Possibly that was why my instructor tried to kill us both. He was making a landing, with me quietly resting in the front seat, when suddenly a Tiger Moth appeared out of nowhere at right-angles to us, fifty feet above the ground; the two planes collided, and ours disintegrated — wings, airscrew, and tail unit flying off in various directions, so that all that was left was the fuselage in which we were sitting, and which itself proceeded to sit down suddenly and heavily on the grass beneath. There was neither time nor height to consider leaping out in mid-air and pulling the release ring of my parachute. I gazed stupidly at the other plane, now poised vertically with smoke pouring from its nose, embedded firmly in Mother Earth. Hastily the pupil who had been flying it solo recovered his wits and slid what seemed a long distance to the ground from the rear seat in which he had been sitting, before bolting towards the horizon at speed. I unclipped my safety harness and climbed out at the same time as my instructor, and got a safe distance from the crashed plane in case it caught fire. As my instructor had already crashed one plane that morning he was grounded for setting a bad example to the pupils. I took my escape for granted, knowing that we were young men with charmed lives.

Not Lloyd, however, the first flier I was to see die. He took off, solo, just ahead of me, and by the time I was airborne he had plummeted into the field where the girl sometimes stood and waved, to whom I waved a gracious gauntleted hand in answer, in accordance with my World War I reading. Lloyd's Moth caught fire as he hung forward in his straps, obviously knocked out, and the plane burned fiercely with flames flickering through dense black oil smoke; it was all over within two minutes, as I circled helplessly. The boy was scraped into a sack and buried, and I wrote my first war poem.

From time to time we acted as ballast, lying across the tailplane to peg the aircraft to earth while its engine was tested, an operation which required full opening of the throttle, which caused the nose to dip and the tail to rise. The tornado hurled back across our bodies by the tiny Tiger Moth's airscrew was negligible, but soon we were to experience the whiplash of the mighty Hurricanes and Spitfires on the same exercise. It was reputed that more than one erk, which was the name for an airman, had been taken aloft inadvertently by a pilot forgetful of his temporary ballast. Manhandling the planes was ritually prefaced by the RAF's version of "One . . . two . . . three . . . Go!" Nobody knew its origin, but we responded to the stirring, if illogical, cry of "Two Six!"

An important part of our instruction was the technique of forced-landing when, some thousands of feet up, the instructor good-naturedly switched off the engine and watched one's reactions. A pilot is never airborne without having in his mind the distance he can glide should the engine suddenly fail, and knowing where he can make an emergency landing. It is part of airmanship, which makes his life safer. Throughout my flying career and ever since on the roads, in exactly the same way, I have remained on the qui vive for the unexpected — a tyre-burst at high speed, some lunatic charging round a bend on the wrong side of the road, another disobeying traffic lights, and so on, being prepared for the necessary evasive action at any moment when the unforeseen actually happens. Any good driver knows roadmanship. Quick reflexes and good coordination help considerably. They are qualities of the fighter-pilot.

We underwent tuition on a gadget called a Link Trainer, housed in a distant shed; it simulated flying conditions and thus enabled assessment of one's control of an aeroplane. It was extremely boring. Link

Trainers were in every distant shed the Air Force possessed and there was no escape from them until ultimately joining a squadron — even operational pilots had to endure them in some places, but the operational flying I was to undertake was to be on remote overseas campaigns, when sheds were usually too distant.

Before leaving Fairoaks we passed a qualifying examination, achieved with some assistance from the invigilators. For example, during the Aircraft Recognition paper the man next to me couldn't identify a Fairey Battle, a twin-seat fighter used for night defence.

"What happened in 1066?" asked the invigilator.

"Hastings, Sir . . . ?"

"Yes, (patiently), the what of Hastings?"

One day my instructor bade me dive after another plane, and into the mirror through which he watched me I registered sufficient pleasure to get myself recommended for fighters, notwithstanding a poor report on my final testing which took place early on the last morning of the course, hard on the heels of a heavy celebration the previous night. I expect he detected my wildness. To be selected for fighterdom was a signal honour, accorded to only five out of the fifty of us on the course. Of the remainder, seven became instructors, three were retired gracefully, and the remainder went on to train as bomber pilots — bus-drivers, we called them.

The five chosen ones regrouped at a Training Pool at Clyffe Pypard, in Somerset, with forty-five potential fighter-boys from other Elementary Flying Schools, where we waited to progress to our next stage, advanced training. I liked the olde-worldlinesse of those Y's but it was the coldest place on earth. The airfield was actually on the edge of a cliff, over which one dived on take-off. On those bitter winter nights we almost perished. Twenty of us slept in a Nissen hut, formed out of innocent corrugated iron sheets bent over a timber frame, the uninsulated shelter heated by a small iron stove in the middle of the floor which was roared up to white heat before we went to bed, fully dressed, with brown quilted flying-suits on top of our clothes. Great layers of heavy grey coarse woollen blankets piled on top of the beds made movement difficult, and contributed little to body heat once the boiler had cooled off after a couple of hours. The hut might have been transported direct from a Siberian prison camp. In three weeks at Clyffe I flew twice; there were a lot of us to very few Tigers, and the weather was foul.

Eventually a posting sent fifty future fighter-pilots to the Advanced Flying School at Tern Hill, in Shropshire, a peacetime RAF station softened by the embellishment of Women's Air Force ladies. There we graduated to Miles Master I's, fiendish aircraft with retractable undercarriages and in-line engines cooled by glycol, a highly inflammable liquid which was forever leaking. The Masters stalled on the slightest provocation, invariably leading to a brutal spin from which it was a struggle to recover. We lost three of our fifty trainees and one instructor that way and had to bury them.

The curriculum was much the same as at Fairoaks, except that everything happened more quickly and violently; Masters cruised at two hundred miles an hour against the Tiger's seventy. We also learnt to fly at night, which never ceased to be highly alarming, and lost a fourth pupil who crashed in flames. That was at a satellite field at Calverley, whose inhabitants had been protesting at the noise we made at night, even though we stopped by midnight. As several of them saw poor old Kennet burn to death the complaints came to a sudden end, as they seemed to realise that we no more liked what we were doing than they did, and thereafter we were brave young men risking our lives to learn the defence and preservation of their cosy little existences. At that stage I had not begun to think of the fighting men, a small percentage of the armed forces and an even smaller one of the total population, as the nation's idiots. Kennet had been a corporal in the Army and had got himself seconded to the RAF because it was considered to be a softer touch. Well, he never even saw action.

The whole of the first three months of 1942 saw interminable snow and ice and we hung around awaiting flying weather, spending a good deal of time playing cards in the large heated room set aside for drying wet clothes. By the end of one week I had won no less than £13 playing poker, more than twenty weeks' pay, but that same night I lost it all and another £2 into the bargain; I vowed I would never again play poker, nor have I.

About two dozen of us slept on iron beds on a gleaming wood floor, each with a scarred tin chest alongside to house our scant possessions. We were responsible not only for making our own beds, in a hospital-like way, but for keeping our own area of floor-space as clean and polished as the brass buttons on our uniforms, and as shiny as our black shoes. My immediate neighbour was a haughty Free Frenchman, one of those who had escaped from his own country, and whose prize possession was a tricouleur, which lived in his tin cupboard alongside a collection of perfumes, deodorants and unguents, applied each morning while the rest of us were washing and showering. Doubtless he also had a bottle of dirt-remover. He was at least twenty years ahead of the After-Shave Lotion market. Sergeant Joli, another Free Frenchman, was a totally different animal, small and cherubic. When drunk, which was most evenings, he stripped and stood on a table and ate wineglasses or swallowed fire; he came from a circus family. Bobby Kerr, a tiny Glaswegian with a large sense of humour and limitless courage, used to pummel the biggest of us in our copious spare time. Deserted by his charm, he was one of those killed in a crash not much later. As the deaths occurred we realised that we were not all immortal, that some might die, though never oneself.

Persistent snow, fog and ice continued to impair the flying programme and twice we were sent home on extended leave, until recalled by telegram after ten or more days. The pattern was unpleasant — it wrecked the momentum of both training and psychological adaptation. The switch to home life was unnerving — if you are flying it has to be done every day. But when the weather still prevented a regular flying schedule we concentrated on ground work, which again was a continuation of what we had been taught at Leuchars and Fairoaks — navigation, aircraft recognition and elementary engineering were absorbed, but guns continued to baffle me. At Tern Hill we added to our exclusive RAF vocabulary, including "I couldn't care less", "Pull your finger out" (which meant "Stop dreaming and get on with what you're supposed to be doing"), "the dreaded end" and "the final curtain" (both meaning getting killed), "shooting a line" (embroidering a tale, or just showing off), "a piece of cake", ("That's easy!"), and "Press on regardless".

The Master I had proved over-lethal and was gradually replaced by the Master III, which had a radial air-cooled engine and was thus less likely to catch fire, and an enlarged rudder, which countered the tendency to spin and made escape from a spin relatively easy. But as there weren't enough Mark IIIs to go round, from time to time we had to take our turn on the treacherous Is, in one of which I executed an inaccurate slow-roll at five thousand feet and flicked into one of those diabolical spins. As the whirling earth rushed up at me I fought to recover — stick fully forward, full opposite rudder to the direction of spin, engine open wide to create a flow of air over the rudder. You couldn't easily get out of a spinning plane but I hadn't enough height left by the time the thought entered my head — I was too busy fighting. The plane eased back into control a few hundred feet above the fields. The charm had not yet deserted me and the dreaded end had failed to claim another victim.

I was quite put off slow-rolling. But the Master I had not yet finished with me, when a little later I embarked on my second-ever solo cross-country flight. By the time I arrived somewhere in Somerset its engine was in doubtful shape. Whilst I phoned back to Tern Hill to report my safe arrival the machine was checked over, titivated, and reported serviceable. We arranged, however, that immediately after take-off I would do a couple of circuits round the airfield as a flight test, and if nothing seemd blatantly amiss I would just press on back to Tern Hill, "regardless." It was a mere hour or so's flying distance away, and off I duly went. When I tested them the magnetos showed a slightly excessive drop and the oil pressure was not as high as it should have been, but those did not quite add up to enough to justify declaring the aircraft unsafe. Foolishly, I set off northwards. Within quarter of an hour the oil pressure had more or less disappeared completely, clouds of black smoke were billowing from under the engine cowling, and the radiator temperature gauge was rising fast; I was rapidly losing height. The sickening stench of glycol told me that the engine coolant was leaking and I knew that the wretched contraption was about to catch fire. Although intensely reluctant to bale out from my warm, comfortable seat, however smoky, I slid the cockpit canopy open and unfastened the safety harness which pinioned me to my seat. I prayed that the parachute would open when I pulled the ripcord. Oil spattering the windscreen made visibility difficult, as I peered desperately for somewhere to force-land. There was nowhere. As I stood up in my seat in order to throw myself over the side the slipstream tore at my helmet and whipped my goggles to the back of my head, lashing me. Then unbelievably there it was — an airfield dead ahead, barely five miles away, and we were absolutely fairly and squarely lined up with a runway.

We were down to two thousand feet, from which height I could not possibly glide those miles; I needed whatever power I could urge from the doomed engine. I nursed it, praying again, this time that it would not burst into flames. I needed only a couple of minutes, but this was my last chance to bale out. I pushed my luck and stayed with the plane. With perhaps ten feet of height left I slammed down the undercarriage and flaps and switched off the engine as we skimmed over the boundary of the airfield. I could see nothing through the clouds of oil smoke now enveloping the plane. As I came to a stop I was literally dragged out of the cockpit by an alert fire crew who had seen my black cloud miles away, gradually approaching, and who had identified it as a plane in distress. They were really on the ball. They placed me in their tender and drove me to the Operations Room. I had landed at a bomber station. They put me up for the night and next morning presented me with an egg, a by now rare and much-prized commodity upon which, black marketeers aside, only privileged operational flyers breakfasted, and then only if doing a business trip that day — rather like the condemned prisoner's last breakfast. Later that afternoon my instructor arrived in another Master to fly me home, and I climbed carefully into the cockpit, cosseting my treasure which I intended showing to the other chaps as evidence of my adventure, but after we had landed back at Tern Hill I absent-mindedly forgot that it was carefully clutched in my left hand, so that it crunched stickily on the side of the fuselage as I hoisted myself out. I fought back the tears as I mopped up the mess.

Next day I managed to fly slap into the middle of the balloon barrage at Crewe. My yelp for help down the intercom woke my instructor who had been taking a quiet nap in the back seat; with great presence of mind he immediately steep-turned the Master to fly back out of the barrage the way we'd come in. That manoeuvre hadn't occurred to me, but he was very decent about my gaffe, for on the way home he got lost and was obliged to descend, physically and spiritually, to the level of Wrexham Railway Station in order to get a pinpoint. That was a task known as "Bradshawing", after the name of the publishers of the railway guide of the time. Although the names of all stations had been painted out so that enemy flyers could not Bradshaw, the platform sign was in large, raised lettering which could perfectly easily be read despite the camouflage. The poor chap died a week later, the instructor to whom a Master I did its usual trick and span him into a large hole in the ground.

We used to besport ourselves in the local pubs most of the boring evenings when we were not flying, to swill pints of watery beer. One of our chaps downed sixteen pints on a sufficiently dull evening, though my record was a mere twelve. It was virtually non-alcoholic and was known as gnat's piss. It was in the pubs that we managed to consort with the locals who were willing to consort with us, which was by no means all of them. I found myself at a party which included a number of married ladies whose husbands were elsewhere, and was shocked beyond description when without provocation or warning one of them set upon me. There was an awful lot of sex-starvation in those days, with husbands away in the Armed Forces, and men from the occupied countries — France, Norway, Poland, Czechoslovakia and so on — separated from their women, so that a general switch-round seemed to occur. Englishmen were sent off to Africa and similar places, while their place was taken by the Poles etcetera and especially by the Americans, newly joined in the hostilities. Some of our men were lucky enough to end up in Australia or South Africa or the United States, there to take the places of those natives who had been sent to England or elsewhere. The theory was that a man fights better away from home, but I doubt whether the distractions of home necessarily outweigh those of worrying about what's going on there in one's absence, especially if one is married; the enormous loosening of sex morality post-war may in part be due to the acknowledgement implicit in that switch-around which went on for six years, a distorted quadrille. Young bachelors were not unduly troubled by the problem.

A Spitfire flew in and did a peach of a landing. A rare bird, we rushed out to inspect it, in time to see the prettiest little doll-like blonde trip out, wearing slacks and sporting the wings of the Air Transport Auxiliary on her tunic. We untrained heroes felt suitably cut-down to size. The Spitfire was itself a feminine-looking little plane, and as deadly as any female of the species. There it stood — an inert, docile and pretty assembly of metal, but quite lifeless, utterly without harm. It was the first I had seen on the ground, where it stood on pert, splayed legs and with a rather cheeky but vastly personable nose, full of fine point. Its designer, Mitchell, was influenced by bird forms, and to me the Spitfire always had something of the prettiness and pertness, as well as the boldness, of the robin. I found myself puzzling over the mystery which allowed the sudden transformation of so dainty and harmless a creature into a highly lethal weapon capable of hurtling destruction through the air at several hundred miles an hour. One minute vital and deadly, the next dead and lifeless. That mystery of metamorphosis has caused me childlike surprise ever since.

A few days later an enormous four-engined Halifax bomber flew in, and out stepped the same blonde doll. In our admiration and awe we paid her charming compliments, but justifiably she was haughty and stayed firmly on her pedestal. We hadn't even got our wings yet.

Towards the end of the course we flew the Hurricane I, an early model with eight machine-guns in the wings. Although we were by now accustomed to flying solo, this was our first pure single-seater. The cockpit felt compact and secure, with a thick armoured plate behind the seat as protection from attack from the rear.

On my first landing I bounced higher than any pilot has ever done before or since; fortunately the Hurricane was a burly bird and shrugged off the indignity with aplomb.

Most of us qualified at the Wings examination, though nearly all had to sit the armaments paper a second time, with a bonus mark of sixty — which was the pass mark. I amassed a bumper total of sixty-seven. Avid to receive the much-sought-after and long-awaited emblem, we expected a grand parade and a bit of hoo-ha commensurate with the occasion; but for some reason the Station Commander was fed up with us at the time, and we simply queued up at the clothing stores where the precious insignia were dished out like so many pairs of service socks, accompanied by the triple chevron which denoted that we were now sergeants. A sweet little WAAF (the acronym for the Women's Auxiliary Air Force) who had befriended me sewed my badges on to my tunic, and I removed the white Under-Training flash from my forage cap. I was a Sergeant-pilot.

I went home on leave feeling more than a little self-conscious, as the Blackpool hotels and boarding houses billeted scores of thousands of raw RAF recruits who daily stamped up and down the forlorn promenade and who gawked in curiosity at a pilot fully-fledged. In the immediate hinterland of the town the cafés buzzed with a scintillating overflow of theatrical people from London, doing their bit for the troops, their war effort enriching the town by way of an unstinted theatricality, and enhancing its natural

34

staginess. The odd, artificial atmosphere was neurotic, a long way removed from Bolton Wakes week, though it seemed to provide an appropriate background for the dramatic quality of my new role. From then on I was continually asked by kindly-disposed civilians, and less kindly soldiers, how many enemy planes I had shot down, and learnt to brush the question aside, leaving an esoteric question-mark rather than an unromantic zero. I became indifferent to the "Brylcreem Boy" appellation given by the Army to airmen, because of what they considered the comparative softness of our living conditions.

Again there was a thinning out, with a number of our Tern Hill men whisked off as instructors and ferry-pilots, but in early summer, 1942, thirty-odd of us returned to Scotland on a final course prior to joining a squadron, at what was called an Operational Training Unit. There we operated as an auxiliary squadron defending the region, and tried to imbibe the finer points of aerial combat under the instruction of men who had operational experience. In the Hurricane II, armed with twelve machine-guns, we learnt to dog-fight, to fly in tight formation including through dense cloud, and to carry out strafing raids. We practised interceptions and deflection-shooting, using a camera-gun which enabled us to study our results on a screen the same evening. Over the sea we fired our guns for the first time, as I held my breath awaiting a mighty explosion, but there was only the slightest rattle behind the engine's roar. For the first time we hobnobbed with men who wore the medal ribbons of the Distinguished

Service Order and Distinguished Flying Cross, and took positive strides away from boyhood. The thing was becoming real. One of them, a Czech who had fought brilliantly in the Battle of Britain, considered that the most important thing in flying was to relax. "You are all tensed up," he commented — "Go into Dundee and get yourself a woman."

We were taught the use of the sun in combat. "Beware of the Hun in the sun" had been a tag familiar since boyhood, and here I was having it dinned into me as a serious tactic of my new profession — in a dogfight one tries to place oneself between the opponent and the sun, so that the opponent is dazzled when searching for his attacker. But dogfighting seemed mostly to consist of trying to get on the other chap's tail by turning in towards him, then by virtue of executing steeper and ever steeper turns you could fire just ahead of him so that he flew into your shells and you had him. Eventually I managed to accomplish the really steep climbing turns which are the essence of dogfighting, and experienced the effect of what we called "G", that is the pull of gravity. In a very tight turn, or indeed in any sudden manoeuvre changing the flying attitude of the machine, the pull of gravity is greatly intensified, the effect being to drain the blood heavily from the top to the bottom part of the body, away from the head into the feet. The eyes are thereby dragged downwards in their sockets, and face muscles and especially mouth pulled bootwards until vision becomes first grey, then black, and failure to ease the manoeuvre leads to swift unconsciousness — the famous "blackout", since misapplied to all manner of mental extravagance. Losing consciousness through the effects of "G", which at one time or another has happened to every fighter-pilot, was not serious, provided there was sufficient height to recover control of the plane once the cause of the excessive "G" was removed. With its pilot temporarily unconscious, an aeroplane itself eases off the intensity of the manoeuvre, and once back to three or four times the pull of gravity (3 or 4 G), consciousness and vision immediately return as the blood flows back to brain and eyes. But the sensation was unpleasant and we quickly became adept at the steepest turns which allowed us to hover on the threshold without blacking out.

An equally unpleasant physical experience resulted from sudden altitude changes. Air density decreases with altitude, so that by the time a pilot has climbed swiftly to, say thirty thousand feet, the air outside his body is considerably less dense than at ground level, whereas that inside his body has lost comparatively little density. The resultant intensification of air pressure inside the body in relation to that outside it has the dramatic effect of making the blood "boil", in the same way as that of a diver who endures the agony of "the bends" if he is too precipitately hoisted to the surface after working in conditions of great pressure deep below the sea's surface. But whereas a diver has the benefit of a decompression chamber to relieve the effect, no such device is available to the fighter-pilot. The effects were felt in reverse, especially in the ear passages, when diving steeply earthwards. They were countered by gulping in air and swallowing hard, and by resisting the stoving-in of the eardrums, due to increasing external pressure, by compressing the lips, pinching the nostrils, and then blowing sharply and steadily down the sealed nose to force equalising air into the passages of the ears, and thus push the pressured drums outwards. In modern aircraft both problems are surmounted by artificially controlling the air pressure in the cockpit and by the use of special clothing.

The long period of training, now over a year, was morally enervating. I had already waited much too long to flex my muscles.

CHAPTER
THREE

Emigration

Stuffed full of inoculations against yellow fever, rabies, typhoid, cholera and you-name-it-we've-got-it, the train journey from Scotland to Blackpool on ten days' embarkation leave, standing the whole way in a corridor and feverish from the injections, was an ordeal. My eventual departure witnessed differing parental valedictions. My sweet Mother, usually so wise, looked calm as she bade me Goodbye, quite possibly for the last time, before addressing me Polonius-wise:

"Take care of yourself." She glanced at my wings. "Don't fly too fast," she continued, "and stay safely near the ground. And don't forget to air your underclothes."

My Father accompanied me to the railway station, Manchester (London Road), Piccadilly, having been flattened on one of those awful 1940 nights when I had been creeping home, and broke down. Curious, when we'd hardly exchanged a dozen words in the preceding seven years. Perhaps that was why.

"Son," he addressed me, having previously decided to do a deal with the Almighty in order to ensure my safe return, "I won't go near a racecourse until you're safely back."

For an inveterate gambler that was quite a premium to pay. I learnt later that he had in fact managed to maintain his abstinence for the best part of a month, by then doubtless confident that the insurance policy had been issued and would not be revoked.

An inhospitable embarkation camp, nor far from Manchester, provided the launching-point for such debauchery as could in the prevailing circumstances be mustered, but there was little heart in it, even though my young brother and I managed to get blind drunk on my last night there. We had no idea where we were being sent, only that it was overseas. For the last time we entrained for Scotland, where in July 1942 at Gourock a horde of uniformed men embarked on to *Ranpura*, an armed merchantman converted into a troopship, whose steerage compartments and decks were littered with hammocks and six-inch naval guns. A to-become-distinguished passenger seventeen years earlier had been the thirty-year-old Robert Graves, en route for Egypt to take up the professorship of Poetry at Cairo University: it had been a gale-ridden voyage which had laid him low. Part of a large convoy, *Ranpura* harboured some twelve hundred souls, the majority soldiers bound for West Africa, but there were rumours that the fifty of us who were pilots were en route for the Western Desert of North Africa. In a tiny cabin, deep below the water line, and with quite inadequate ventilation, fifteen of us were crammed behind a door on which the raised inscription, "Six Native Stewards", had been clumsily painted out. It was war time, and at least we were off at last, bound for somewhere, and as we steamed down the Clyde and round the Isle of Arran my thoughts became unsoldierly as I accepted for the first time the reality that I might never again see family and home. What seemed sad was that they might never again see me, for I would not be over-bothered if dead. I knew by now that flying was inherently dangerous — I had already seen several deaths and had myself used up no less than three lives. With enemy action added, the mixture was potentially lethal. It was all obviously a matter of luck, but I never for one moment doubted mine; I had already proved myself a survivor. Jones, a large, hefty and aggressive Cockney, actually wept openly, confiding to me that he was illegitimate but had been shown so much kindness by his foster-parents that he was prostrated by being parted from them. Perhaps it was worse for him than for us legits. Later he wangled a grounding (that is, being taken off flying) and was posted back home. For all his ostensible toughness he was as soft as butter. That taught me something important.

I turned my back on home and looked ahead with no small excitement to the adventure of travel and the unknown future. Like the vast majority of us, it was my first ever trip abroad. But the Atlantic and I did not get on; we did not get on at all. Down in the bowels of the monster *Ranpura*, in close proximity to the engine rooms, the stench of diesel oil and the throbbing of the mighty engines combined with the vessel's corkscrewing to affect my equilibrium, rendering me seasick for five long, miserable days; sick half-a-dozen times a day and nauseated the whole time, twenty-four hours incessantly each of those endless days. The motion never relented, the stink of oil was continuous, and the throbbing vibrated through my wracked, retching body day and night, giving me a perpetual blinding headache. I could not eat, though encouraged to crunch dried bread and swallow water so as to provide something to sick up. I spent as much time as possible on deck where at least there was the air denied to us in the deep, dismal, native stewards' den, watching the other glaucous vessels of the slow convoy, *Ranpura*'s protégés, until the arrival of four destroyers which were to remain with us for most of the journey, *Ranpura* dropping astern as tail-end watchdog. As we staggered over the awful ocean the other ships seemed to stand still whilst the destroyers raced round their charges in a great flurry of confident bow wave and wake. I found a spot at the stern where I could lean over and puke in reasonable privacy, and between that and writing my second war poem I studied the beautiful fluoresecence of our wake. Most mornings the six-inch guns were fired with great wallops which frightened me out of my supersensitive wits. After those first ghastly days I adjusted to the sea-rhythm and began to eat food which was ineffably superior to that to which we were accustomed in beleaguered England. We had fresh white bread every day, a luxury we had almost forgotten.

We played cards on deck or in our dungeon, and took turns to sleep alongside the only ventilator. As we moved west into mid-Atlantic and south towards the Equator, the weather steadily became hot until we could no longer survive below decks, and only descended to the cabin for clothes. The climb down from the sweet sea air along iron stairways, scrambling over bulkheads, the vibration and smell from the engine-room, deterred the venture unless necessity compelled, and the decks became littered each evening with our mattresses. It was during that period that I was subjected to a second homosexual approach, from one of the crew, incensed perhaps by the sight of our increasingly nude bodies as we drew nearer the central girdle. From time to time we participated in a chaotic boat drill which I hoped would never have to be implemented in reality. Sailor-fashion, we exercised by swift solemn lion cage paces up and down our patch of Other Ranks' deck, back and forth, back and forth.

We voyaged tranquilly through the unwarlike days, until one evening we saw with naked eyes that we were being tailed by a surfaced submarine, a speck of burnished metal on the distant glittering horizon. As the destroyers went charging off to investigate I fully expected that in its depleted state of protection the convoy would be attacked whilst they were away after the decoy; but nothing happened until they returned, to pronounce that the sub was a friendly Dutchman which had come up for air or to charge its batteries or whatever submarines come up for in the evenings. By now we were in dolphin water, and they sported around and among the convoy, oblivious of our serious mission, as did the random flying-fish, flopping in and out of the sparkling sea and telling us that we really were in tropical latitudes. It became still hotter. Half of the convoy broke away with a couple of the destroyers to shove off for the Americas; we had been executing large zigs and zags through the Atlantic to confuse the enemy, feinting from time to time towards Central America, and now the departing half was off up to the United States while the rest of us pushed across to West Africa at increased speed.

One morning, some earlier than usual explosions from the mighty guns brought a white RAF Sunderland flying-boat crashing into the sea. The crew were picked up intact but — foolish fellows that they were — they had had the temerity to approach the convoy out of the rising sun without sufficiently identifying themselves, which had proved too much for the trigger-itchy sailors. I had good cause to remember that lesson not all that much later. But at least the presence of the Sunderland indicated that we were within a few hundred miles of land, and a few days later, amid great excitement from the troops leaning over the ship's rails, the African coastline showed up on the horizon. Low and fuzzy, rich green woody curls on low-lying hills, the water as calm as you like, deep emerald opalescence spattered with thick jade-like clusters. For slow hours we seemed to steam parallel with the still-distant coast without getting any closer, presumably awaiting a tide; the suspense became unbearable. Then all of a rush we swung shorewards and in no time straight into a beautiful harbour, where the fuzzy curls stormed into lofty jungle, and low over-verdant hills stretched upwards on three sides in impressive grandeur. Paddles flashing like spears in the sun brought out a fleet of dugout canoes ripping wakes through the iridescent water, and we were surrounded by an escort of white teeth gleaming in grinning black faces, and could hear the excited jabber of three naked Freetown harbour-beggars arrived to greet and entertain us. As the diesels slackened their drive and the engine-throb abated, the men stood up in their bobbing boats yelling thickly, "Hello Jock!", "What about a Liverpool tanner (sixpenny piece), Tommy!", "Give us a Glasgow sixpence, Mac!" For them the occasion was by no means a premiere performance. As the silver coins span from the rail the boatmen dived deep into the water to recover them in an amazing display of aquatic acrobatics. As the flow of sixpences ebbed, pennies became sufficient to justify the astonishing dives.

The soldiers disembarked, leaving only the crew and the RAF men; although a day and a half in the harbour we were not allowed ashore, then we were off again towards our unknown destination. Porpoises and flying-fish, and limitless acres of aimless ocean impaled on the thrashing screws until land appeared again and we were at Takoradi on the Gold Coast. As the sudden dusk cascaded we were ferried ashore in tenders, then our feet touched Africa — the dark, magic, stimulating continent where ebony night was waiting to envelop us. It was stuffily hot, crickets chirruped unrestrained greetings as we clambered aboard lorries to whine off down a tarmac road, our headlights picking out mysterious black figures among shadowed trees; black faces on otherwise familiar advertisement hoardings came as a shock — did negroes really drink Ovaltine? and polish their shoes with Cherry Blossom? The summer night air seemed aglow with firefly twinkle, and there was no doubting that we were in an entirely new world.

At the same time as we were unceremoniously dumped into a hutted transit camp we learnt that we were bound for Nigeria. Next day we wandered into Takoradi's blinding heat, feeling and undoubtedly looking quaint in the weird khaki drill outfits we had brought with us from Britain — a jacket known as a bush-shirt, coarse cotton shirts, short (knee-length) and long (ankle-length) trousers, the latter with a dromedary hump at the back for attaching braces to; and mighty Empire-builder pith helmets designed by one of our famous 19th-century explorers. The kit was completed by long, thick stockings intended for Polar use. With our pink knees, bright red faces and noses peeled by the sea-breezes and sun we must have looked hilarious — fair game for those on the lookout for obvious sprogs from Home. For the most part the Africans were delightful, unspoilt children, difficult to reconcile with the urbane princes encountered during my brief university career. Apart from them, the only negro I had ever seen was the poor shrammed creature who swept the Salford streets with a giant brush, and for whom I did not know what to do. Awed, I watched footballers kicking heftily with bare feet and tackling with total confidence opponents shod in traditional hobnails. I marvelled at happy mammies swathed in robes dyed indigo which covered strapping thighs. In disbelief I wandered past stalls marketing practically everything under the sun but none of which was identifiable. I admired the erect bodies of young women carrying heavy baskets of fruit and vegetables on strong heads, with one slender black arm held elegantly in support. I reeled at the sight of a young grandee, a veritable vision in panama hat, saffron shirt, scarlet pullover, azure shorts, purple socks, and white-and-tan shoes, who found the sun strong and wore sunglasses and carried a parasol. I gave pennies galore to young boys and girls who followed us calling, "Dash me a penny, massa."

Meandering by chance into a village growing under palm-trees beside a stream I beheld a scene straight out of "Sanders of the River" — wispy-bearded elders seated sagely beneath a plaited awning, mammies beating out washing in the stream, a young mother laughingly rinsing her screaming piccaninny free of Palmolive soap-suds, children shyly approaching then following me, the menfolk absent doing something, or nothing. "You dash me, Massa," suggested one emboldened lad, "banana," pointing to a lusciously-fronded clump of trees. He sold me a bunch of six for a penny, when you couldn't get them for love or money at home. I ate all six. Young girls plaited each other's hair to eliminate the natural kinks. One of them shinned up a palm to hack down a coconut with a machete, whittled deftly here and there then handed it to me to drink. She refused the penny I offered her; but her young brother took it swiftly enough. It was a beautiful occasion, and I left the party at its height. Down on the beach the African surf rolled lazily in, bobbing the moored dugouts and agitating at their gaudy paintwork. I was particularly taken with "H M Save God The King", which measured three-and-a-half metres by one-and-a-half.

A week later we boarded *New Northland*, a pretty little eighteen hundred-ton coaster, which whistled us down to Lagos in two and a half days. It was a sunny, leisured voyage, without six-inch guns or seasickness, and seemed utterly disconnected from anything to do with war. In no time we were in another transit camp at Yaba, near Apapa Airport, on the outskirts of the Nigerian capital, a large, flourishing and industrious place full of warehouses, mission schools, churches and trees. A wide, red earth road ran through the middle of the camp, ascending a short hill atop which sat a white church with a tolling bell. The whole environment was airless. We met the permanent staff of the camp, who were not reluctant to communicate their local lore. Several of us had long since felt the lack of female company, so "What do you do for women?" we asked pointedly. They looked perplexed.

"There are thousands all round you," they said.

"Yes, but they're black!" (What parochial prigs we were.)

"Look, mate — they may look black the first week you're here but by the second they'll be khaki; and the third week they'll be as white as you are!"

That proved fairly accurate.

The two prevalent tribes of the area were Hausa and Yoruba, the former tall, thin and with fine noses, reputedly of Semitic origin, warrior/traders, equally adept with spear or cash, and who plied their wares round the camp. We bought lion-skins, carved bone bric-á-brac, ornate knives beaten out of petrol tins, and decorated leather objects. The Yoruba were farmers, their faces scarred with markings, three horizontal surmounted by three vertical lines inflicted at an early age as a means of identification in the event of theft by raiding tribes. The scars were caused by knife cuts into which a bluish dye was rubbed. Before the cuts healed they were reopened a number of times to ensure good, deep, ineradicable scars.

We travelled into Lagos on small buses called "mammy-cars," sitting on slatted seats. Two young men were discussing life at large until one of them got too big for his boots, so humiliating the other by his superior knowledge that the latter burst out angrily:

"Why, you dam' nigger! You never been go for 'Merica!"

This awful insult was followed by a moment's shocked silence. Then came a cutting riposte.

"I been done go for 'Merica! What you know 'bout Noo York, huh?"

Again a knife-edged interval, when the rest of us on the bus held our breath.

"Noo York! NOO York!! You ever been go for Philadeph'la? Huh?"

The question was too crushing and brought a swift and savage end to the dialogue. Fisticuffs ensued, and I was faintly surprised that the blood which ran from the nose of one of the combatants was the same colour as mine.

In the town we ate at canteens set up to cater for the passing troops, run by hot-blooded middle-aged white ladies helped by black boys, against whom they rubbed up too frequently and too obviously. The sage old-timers advised us that while the tropics thin a white man's blood and enervate him, they rouse unknown passions in white women; my stay in Nigeria, which happened to last three weeks, did not prove too enervating. The canteen lads were largely the product of mission schools; they seemed sullen and unfriendly, and by our standards semi-educated; possibly they became top civil servants. At that stage I never queried my right as an Englishman to make myself at home in a foreign country, perhaps because of the respect to which my pink skin, polite ways, moustache and purse seemed to entitle me. A future politician must surely have been the thin, angry drunk who marched his robes across my inoffensive path, muttering fierce unintelligible words which were translated for me as "Out of my way, white man!" It was rumoured that a white man's body was daily hauled out of the harbour waters, and certainly the tom-toms which beat throughout the hot nights, accompanied by wild chanting and blood-curdling shrieks, lent credence to the yarn. Undoubtedly black magic and witchcraft played an important sociological role in urban African life in those days. I wonder to what extent they entered into the life of the desperate little barefooted man in ragged shirt and shorts, who accosted me in the street one evening with the words, "Excuse me, sir, I am a comedian." Admittedly that was a pretty effective punchline, and like the wedding guests I was duly stopped in my tracks.

"Sir," he continued, "I beseech you to read my verses," and he produced a sheaf of poetry which politeness or shyness or simply fellow-feeling compelled me to glance through. It was real William McGonagall stuff, but what he meant by "comedian" was obviously the opposite of tragedian — he did not set out to make people split their sides, rather to please by lilting lyric. As an Englishman, could I not, he implored, introduce his work to the great and famous London Public where it could be declaimed, not necessarily by himself (he was not interested in fortune, merely fame) but by some actor of note? As soothingly as I could I explained that the London theatres had more or less closed down since the war started, and I was myself on my way to eastern Africa. Poor little man; how well I knew the desperation which had driven him to accost the influential sergeant-pilot, accustomed to the lofty seats of privilege, the familiar of personages of power.

Our mornings, scheduled for aimless loitering within the boundaries of the camp, were enlivened by the daily visits of Victoria, a little Hausa beauty aged twelve, all impish confidence. She used to turn up on our verandah, bearing on her little head a huge basket of fruit which she proceeded to sell at exorbitant prices; but she threw in songs and dances which enchanted us, and we were her slaves and would have done anything for her. She spoke not a single word of English, but she didn't need to — she had the Scheherezade mix of sexiness, intelligence and perspicacity about men that has never failed to entrance me. One of her songs-cum-dance ended with the words, "Ya Ya, Ba-tu-rei!" meaning "Oh, oh, you soldiers!" and I gathered that the whole performance was gently mocking — she knew what soldiers really wanted, and it wasn't war!

At twenty-one a day is still a long time and a week of idleness an eternity, especially as we had grown used to living from day to day, and we seemed to be at Yaba for ever, watching the lizards lithely waddling about their sun-drenched business and doing nothing positive. Then one day Victoria's young sister turned up in her place, and we learnt that Victoria would visit us no more — she had married the man to whom she had been betrothed since she was eight.

The time arrived for our departure by air for Khartoum, across the Congo jungle, Africa's heart, and I was made to accept a juju which would make me stay in Nigeria for ever. I wouldn't have minded one bit, for it was a lotus-eating existence and the heat was suiting me well, with no perceptible thinning of the blood. Self-consciously, yet with proper solemnity, I performed my part in an esoteric ceremony, dipping and stirring into a broken egg a strange device, consisting of a handle of rough-barked wood into each end of which had been driven the point of a steel rod bent round into an arc, and around which were wrapped fragments of lionskin studded with the teeth of I knew not what creature — perhaps some missing English serviceman. I had at the same time to mutter something three times and spit over one or other of my shoulders. Next day we reported at Apapa Airfield, just along the way, and with mixed feelings I heaved my baggage on to the weighing-scale; there was no doubt that some of the misgiving was related to my incipient participation in a war which had receded into an increasing distance. Next day a Lockheed troop-carrier flew in and a file of men trailed out to board her, but the weight of our belongings had been miscalculated and five of us were left behind. Another Lockheed was due an hour later (they shuttled between Apapa and Khartoum) but failed to arrive. We spent the night at Yaba and next day our Lockheed was waiting for us. Then we waited for it, because it was unserviceable. Hours passed. We returned to spend the night at Yaba. A further technical hitch on the third successive day had me twitching, and in my nervousness I began to hear tom-toms behind the shoulder over which I had spat. I considered throwing the juju away, but that might make matters even worse. The situation was alarming.

The first of the Lockheeds arrived back from Khartoum. Four days late we boarded her and were airborne, swinging wide of Lagos harbour and round on course for Kano in the Nigerian hinterland. A few hours later we circled for the landing, and I took in the red mud buildings of the ancient walled town, baked like the mud in Congo torpor, before the plane settled on to terra firma to refuel. As we took off again, this time for Maiduguri, close to French Equatorial Africa which I knew only from the exciting postage stamps of childhood, I recollected the words of the juju: "Always you stay for Nigeria!" We were still in Nigeria, and I was breathless as the Lockheed stuttered into the air. Even then it was not over, for there was still a night to spend on Nigerian soil, before another take-off. It was a wretched night, too, in a makeshift mess lit by dim paraffin lamps, the tablecloths grey with mosquitoes. We retired early, but sleep was impossible in the hot, steaming night, the juju possessing my imagination. All sorts of things could still happen to prevent my leaving Nigeria, and I had no relish for the prospect of being buried alive there, or thrown into a harbour, deep stabwounds and all, my teeth yanked out for the next batch of jujus.

Early the following morning we soared beyond the witch-doctor's clutches and later that day landed at El Fasher in French Equatorial Africa, the last stop before Khartoum. Alongside flew a bunch of Hurricanes painted the colour of sand, destined, like us, for the Western Desert of North Africa. A regular service of Hurricanes and Lockheeds on that rough equatorial route enabled supplies to reach the Allied forces then beleaguered outside Alexandria, the Mediterranean being still Mussolini's Mare Nostrum and denied to our use — it had been the graveyard of too many Allied supply ships and men.

Khartoum's heat was searing — you could literally fry eggs in the sand if you felt so disposed. We were greeted by those of our draft who had flown on earlier, by then ensconced comfortably in the large RAF Station which was to be our pitch until the arrival of another plane to take us on to Cairo. Apart from the heat, our chief point of interest was a herd of donkeys braying day and night round the corner, seemingly never off heat; the sight of the males was awe-inducing, until one worked out that by virtue of the asinine anatomy life would quickly come to an end without the very extended male lines of communication. Sudanese servants, sweeping around silent and dignified in thin white robes, were unmistakably kin with the Hausas we had left several thousand miles behind. By the swimming pool near the Mess, moths and a myriad other insects swirled in the beam of the electric lamps lighting its borders — a mad, whirling column of them from the ground upwards became another principal distraction. During the day camels swayed along the trails on the camp's outskirts, loftily superior beasts, ugly as sin and bad-tempered as Satan, with disdainful long-lashed eyes and dirty brown tombstone teeth, chewing wearily at their cuds and spattering the trails and themselves with their droppings. They kicked like mules, only with all four legs.

We discarded our absurd empire-builders' pith helmets in favour of the humdrum glengarry, but still looked pretty raw material. En route for Cairo again, we stopped down at Wadi Natrun, a hundred miles from Wadi Halfa, and reputedly the hottest — or perhaps it is the wettest — place on earth. At the Temples of the Pharaonic Kings, Luxor, at our next stop, with appearances heavily against us we became the latest victims of the local professionals, who unloaded quantities of worthless "jewellery" on us at mad prices, scarabs by the thousand, priceless irreplaceable antiques newly scavenged from the prolific temple tombs. And so up the valley of the snaking Nile, green-margined amid a vast arid desert, until somebody spotted the Gizeh pyramids and the Sphinx, and we knew that Cairo was there. To land at Heliopolis airfield meant flying over that great and bustling city where the Nile in expansive mood was spanned by many bridges, and green parks and racecourses were generously interspersed among tall blocks of shops, offices and apartments, gleaming in the bleaching African sun. At yet another transit camp, at Almaza on the city's outskirts, we were undignifiedly poured into a deep pool of wasting aircrew waiting to join squadrons, over twelve hundred men in all, meantime living in thoroughly bad conditions at the most inefficiently organised station I was to encounter during my five and a half years' service.

Despite the heat, which was much to my liking, dry and without the humidity of our summer, Almaza was a rude shock. The camp was presided over by a fat Australian who looked like an ill-tempered and unfunny Oliver Hardy; he was universally hated, not least by his many compatriots in the aircrew pool. Each morning he paraded his vast army of vassals in the sand, to tell them what worthless, dangerous, imbecile creatures they were, and to warn them that their hearts would be broken before his own. It was difficult to conjecture why anyone might want to break his fat heart, but we were to a man outraged at the way he conducted himself towards a group of highly-trained flying-men. He was what was known to us as a wingless wonder, a chairborne warrior — opprobrious terms for Air Force people who did not fly. Some eighteen months later, he was incapacitated permanently by a dedicated fellow-Australian. He earned the camp the obvious nickname of Alcatraz.

Now part of the populous suburb of Heliopolis, it was an area of several acres of soft sand fronted by a tarmac road, and enclosed within a perimeter of barbed wire, just inside which stood wooden huts that constituted the administrative offices, messes and quarters of the permanent staff; not a few of them were infected by the example of their gallant Commanding Officer. Down the sandy slope a couple of hundred tents were set out geometrically to provide shelter for the aircrew pool, and to one side of them a row of corrugated iron constructions provided what the Services called "Ablutions," closets and washing facilities of a primitive order. Six of us shared a tent covering a floor area roughly twelve feet (three and a half metres) square. Our furniture consisted of a rough straw palliasse laid out in the sand, underneath which we placed such articles of our kit as could withstand being laid upon. Our kitbags and other accoutrements were wedged between the palliasses. As the Mess was some hundreds of yards of sweaty going up the soft slope, we kept our metal water bottles filled, and preferred to supplement an inadequate diet at restaurants in the city; by now we were paid the handsome sum of £3 a week. "Shahi-wallahs" sold us cups of unpleasant tea and soft drinks of doubtful origin, and within three days the whole lot of us started suffering from a mild but disconcerting dysentery. Everyone had to go through it; it was a necessary initiation.

It was September 1942, beautiful English summer weather at its best, but in Cairo a distinct malaise was evident. The enemy was at the gate, El Alamein, and the less confident shopkeepers quickly stopped giving you the tiny cup of greenish tea to which the first customer of the day was entitled, instead openly replacing their photographs of Churchill, Roosevelt and King George VI with those of Hitler and Mussolini. The Army was blaming the RAF for the latest defeat inflicted by Rommel, which had brought his armies into the Nile Delta, within an hour's drive of Alexandria. The RAF, poor innocent creatures, thought it must be something to do with bad generalship. The Anzacs, Australian and New Zealand soldiers, stationed at Ma'adi on the far edge of Cairo, berated the Pommie bastards at large, who in turn vented their wrath on the politicians who, after all, had started the whole thing and held the purse- and other strings. And so it went on, low morale manifest everywhere and communicating itself to the Egyptians, whose demeanour was one of scarcely veiled hostility. For the first time it dawned on me that our position in that foreign land was secured less by goodwill or cash than by force of arms, a cogent persuader when all has been said and done.

King Farouk thought the time had come to throw in his hand openly with the Axis powers, who had been his pre-war advisers, but his palace was promptly surrounded by British tanks to back up a corrective visit by our ambassador, Miles Lampson. But the bootblacks on the wide, tree-lined Cairo avenues became more and more aggressive, and hurled their blackening liquid at our clean trousers with increasing abandon.

Cairenes seemed to fall into three groups — the inordinately wealthy riding in large black cars and living in palaces, who conversed principally in French, Italian or Greek; shopkeepers who aped them, albeit at a less flamboyant level; and the vast masses who flocked in countless hordes through the streets, a dirty fly-ridden agglomeration, desperately poor and beggarly, publicly expectorating and defecating their wretched lives away in between soliciting alms, their only possession their long flowing robe, the gelabeia.

A crowd collects more quickly in Cairo than anywhere in the world, with literally thousands of crowd-makers available at the drop of a hat at any street corner or city square. They seemed to pop up through the broken pavements. Rent-a-mob was invented there. The preponderant bootblacks were coarse boys, polluted both by their vocation and their patrons, from whom they learnt the less widely used words of the English language. Taking a tip from my hero's book, *The Seven Pillars of Wisdom*, I taught myself how to retaliate in their own language, so that when one day one of their number whose offer to polish my shoes I had politely declined turned away and shouted "Ya Kalb" (meaning "Dog!"), I was able to respond enthusiastically in Arabic to let him know that he was the son of no less than seventy dogs, and a black whore. His reaction was to rush away screaming in umbrage.

Largely because of the great, jostling crowds, Cairo was dynamic as well as vivid; trams clanged raucously down wide avenues flanked by brightly lit well-stocked shops and restaurants, with cafés, cinemas, dancehalls, hotels, streetlights, cabarets and gardens interspersed. Policemen in white dealt dispassionately with police problems — brothels, motorists, moneylenders, civilians of French, Greek, Italian and Levantine extraction, camels, buses, bicycles, pimps and touts. Guides, photographers, beautiful raven-haired girls and black-robed peasant women in heavy veils mingled with soldiers, sailors and airmen from Britain, Australia, New Zealand, South Africa, India, Poland and many of the countries occupied by Nazi Germany. Red-tabbed and red-necked generals strode with sticks past conjurors, air marshals with gold trimmings past beggars, sergeants and privates dallied with bootblacks and belly dancers, blue-eyed admirals patronised newsvendors — all kaleidoscopically shifting the pattern of the huge, amorphous, restless, raucous, fez-ridden, fly-infested city that was Cairo. Turkish coffee, cheap jewellery, luxurious clothes, beautiful handbags of crocodile and lizard skins, dark eyes, horse-drawn jalopies, red tarbouches, the tang of human and equine excreta, bedbugs, gin n fizzes — the aromatic and stifling fragrance of a vibrant metropolis where children with fly-filled eyes squinted half blind with awful glaucoma, never bothering to brush away the tormenting insects; where gulli-gulli men performed magical legerdemain against the noise and rhythm of gharries lugged by broken-backed hacks with distended bellies, from which they blew back immoderate amounts of wind in a steady stream at their uncomplaining passengers; where the clamorous trams were ridden inside and out by hordes of gelabeia-clad men whose babble drowned the signal-horns of the hapless conductors — those were coveted trophies; where the hot sun scorched unopposed throughout cloudless days, and glittering star-filled skies lit the romantic eastern night. Over all the city there hung the smell of excreta withered by eternal sun and pulverised by hot breezes from the surrounding deserts, drifting like invisible dust to sting the nostrils acridly.

We revelled in the sensuous indulgence of protracted shaving in the barbers' shops, then our faces rubbed with an ice block to tighten the stretched skin — a luxury marred only by the barber's overwhelming garlic exhalation. A veil of security descended on the goings-on at Alamein, while we wilted in boredom at Almaza, all impetus long since lost. One of our pilots, a harmless, amiable little fellow, had his face bashed askew by the knuckledusters of a frustrated soldier, the only time I have seen a man with his mouth running vertically up and down his battered face. We refused filthy pictures hissed at us from street corners. I found an agreeable French restaurant, Le Petit Trianon, where

I majored from egg and chips on to succulent omelettes. We abandoned our palliasses, finding it more comfortable to sleep in the sand, scooping out hollows for hip and shoulder, and building a small swelling for the head. In my turn I succumbed to dysentery and lay in the sand with a raging fever, awake one long night without water, so that I drank the rusty remnants at the bottom of a stale water-bottle. After four days I was on my feet shakily. We were sick of Almaza, but there was still no news from Alamein and no sign of our leaving. The camp was as full and hot as a boiled egg. Cairo palled. We bought fly-whisks and crêpe-soled chukka boots, known as brothel-creepers, and slinky American khaki slacks of exquisite sea-island cotton. It was only later that I learnt how they came to be available from the street vendors, and how large quantities of military stores and supplies of every description, from food to clothing, from armaments to engine parts, from liquor to vehicles, were "liberated" by unscrupulous storekeepers, British officers as well as NCOs and men, and sold for personal gain to local dealers. It was not to be long before we became victims of that dishonesty.

I searched out a room where I could spend my ample free time in privacy, a commodity now greatly missed. It was in an ancient widow's flat in Heliopolis, furnished and with a cool balcony, for £1 a week. The plump jovial man from the estate agency, Cesare, became a friend. In between writing reams of bad poetry, my sanity was preserved during the ensuing weeks by the hospitality of his home, a Coptic Christian household of whom only his sister, Michelle, mattered.

At eighteen she was simply gorgeous but, regrettably, engaged to Leon, a captain in the Egyptian army, and they were mad about each other. Michelle was the brimming incarnation of sheer, bubbling happiness, but unlike Cesare and Leon she didn't speak a word of English or French, and the conversation was interspersed with her anguished Arabic cries of "Ya-ani, ya-ani?" — "What does it mean?" She was gay, vivacious and uninhibited, vivid and desirable, adored and adorable; her bright, intelligent eyes enchanted me. Cesare spoke French as well as Arabic and we conversed in the former, rather he monologued, pausing every now and then to enquire, "C'est juste, non?" and then prattling on without waiting for an answer. They took me to the Cercle Français where I mixed with civilians, and to parties in other apartments in the large block where they lived. I was an object of some curiosity and I think they were embarrassed by my service shorts, but their amusement was cut short by my description of our Alcatraz conditions, Michelle throwing up her hands in horror and exclaiming "Ya habibi!"

By now we were old sweats, our knees were brown, and our money contained nothing English. As we started to harmonise with our environment, the heat bouncing off the sand and pavements became as refreshing as a spring shower at home, and I threw away my cumbersome Service sunglasses. Anti-aircraft guns opened fire on German bombers which from time to time appeared over Cairo. Within seconds of the first warning siren every shop was shuttered and there wasn't a soul to be seen, except for the British servicemen continuing their aimless mooching. With the "All Clear" the process was swiftly reversed and the place came to life like an electric light switched on. Raided one evening at Almaza, silver searchlights caught and held the enemy bomber, clearly identifiable as a Heinkel 111, while ack-ack guns blasted energetically. As the raider was directly overhead, the flak descended round and among our tents, and we were sheepishly exposed to the falling shrapnel which we could hear clattering on the corrugated iron roofs of the neighbouring ablutions. We stood erect, to make ourselves as thin as possible and gain maximum protection from our steel helmets, but I was very conscious of my shoulders and backside sticking out. What a place to get a lump of shrapnel. We cheered as the bomber was shot down, tumbling in flames into the desert alongside.

We learnt the necessary Arabic words for: "Go away!"; "Girl"; "I'm broke"; "Mind your backs"; "I regret that in my present financial circumstances I am unable to accede to your entirely reasonable request for alms"; "Where is my baggage?"; "Thank you"; "Please"; "Never mind!"; and one splendid expression which literally translated means: "Tomorrow, perhaps, later on, when the apricots ripen." "Maaleesh", or "Never mind!", was essential, being engrained in Egyptian philosophy since time immemorial, and perhaps psychologically sounder than our own RAF "I couldn't care less!" The "Maaleesh" attitude was universal and at times we were infected by it. The extended holiday which had started with the Gourock sea-tour was decently approaching its end, my excitement at acknowledging the fact being a compound of fear and the desire to test my flying ability. I was glad that nobody had asked how many enemy planes I had shot down.

CHAPTER
FOUR

Acclimatisation

At El Ballah, a dusty airfield near the Suez Canal, half-a-dozen of us were put through our paces by a handful of veterans. It was more than three months since we had flown, other than as passengers, and I was jerky and nervous. We practised dogfighting and ground attack in Hurricanes which consistently overheated; they performed considerably less well in the heat, and because they carried four heavy twenty-millimetre cannons in place of the twelve lighter-weight .303 machine-guns of the earlier marks we had flown at home. Outside the Nile Valley, Egypt is a series of deserts, and we settled down to flying conditions which were to become familar. Word filtered through of Montgomery's Alamein success, and of the deaths of two or three of our draft who had joined squadrons ahead of us. After a few days we were flown to an operational standby unit at Wadi Natrun, in the Western Desert, not far from Alamein, where we had a Hurricane each and flew every day, under the command of "Nipper" Boyce, a delightful New Zealander who wore the ribbon of the Distinguished Flying Cross, awarded for having shot down six

German aircraft. He taught us a lot about the ins and outs of desert flying, especially the need to oversee the correct servicing of our planes. In that climate, a loosely screwed wing or fuselage panel impaired the performance of the Hurricanes by as much as ten miles an hour, and we took pains to ensure that the airframe was as sleek as possible. Even so, the matt camouflage paint represented a loss of five miles an hour in relation to a plane with its metal fuselage bare and polished, but that was an unavoidable sacrifice.

As soon as airborne, and again up to the final preparation for landing, the canopy which slid over the cockpit was kept closed, a sweltering experience in the African heat, because when open it reduced speed by as much as fifteen miles an hour, which was a large percentage of our maximum. Sliding the canopy back immediately before landing caused the nose to buffet sharply downwards, corrected by trimming the elevators back by a turn on a wheel housed on the left side of the cockpit. As the hood was opened there was also a sudden blast as the airstream whipped one's goggles from their resting place on the helmet forehead with alarming violence, so that they hammered frenzedly at the back of one's head; but it helped alert the pilot to the intense concentration called for by landing, perfection at which demanded accurate coordination of several factors — within inches of the ground the plane had to be eased into the stalled position, nose up and tail down, but at a speed when the flow of air over the wings was insufficient to provide the pressure beneath and the suction above which together constitute lift. With accurate performance by the pilot the plane would settle gently on to earth, the impact cushioned by its residual forward speed.

The ideal landing was on three points — the two wheels and the skid or wheel at the tail end. After perhaps a few hundred landings, perfection could be achieved almost as a matter of course. As the plane remained in the stalled, three-point position, its long nose obscured all forward vision, so that to taxi a single-engined plane required zigzagging along and looking over the side at where one was going to. Night-landings were difficult because the flarepath which indicated the landing strip was along its left-hand side, and could only be seen by looking over the left side of the cockpit at the moment when the flares were actually being passed, at a speed of some ninety miles an hour — nothing could be seen ahead because the plane was in the three-point stalling attitude. The problem could be overcome by a "wheel" landing, normally used only in conditions of strong cross-wind which drifted a plane sideways when it was in the three-point, stalled attitude. The principle was literally to fly the plane on to the ground with its tail at the same level as the wings, which could only be done by a fast approach at a speed some ten miles an hour above stalling speed. The Hurricane stalled at about eighty-five miles an hour, so that a "wheels" approach was at ninety-five miles an hour, which meant using up a good deal more runway (the Hurricane's brakes were poor) — but one had lateral control, by use of the rudder, and so avoided being drifted sideways. The rudder, and indeed all the other controls, only operate if there is an adequate flow of air over their surfaces. Modern airplanes are invariably tricycle-undercarriaged, which means that they take off, land and taxi with tail up, and therefore always under control; they can do this because of their powerful brakes and other slowing-down systems, such as reverse thrust and, in the case of some fighters, the deployment of a tail-parachute.

The thrill of taking off never varied. Having run up and tested the engine and mechanical controls, the seat was lowered by a simple hand-lever, goggles and radio-cum-oxygen mask adjusted, the aircraft standing athwart the runway's extremity to enable clear vision of the approaches. Swinging round to point down its length, the throttle was steadily opened to roar the great engine, spinning the airscrew at thousands of revolutions a minute as it drew the hurtling plane forward in increasing acceleration, bumping ever more gently as the airstream lifted the tailplane and flying speed was attained. A glance at the airspeed indicator corroborated the feeling in the seat of one's pants, and at ninety-five miles an hour the elevators on the tailpane were trimmed slightly forward to stop the nose pointing too high, the plane was allowed to ease itself off the ground, and as it did so, the hydraulically-operated undercarriage was lifted by a handle. The throttle was adjusted to reduce boost, the airscrew's pitch was adjusted by a lever which reduced the angle of incidence of its blades, the elevator control was trimmed gently back, and as the machine climbed

69

smoothly heavenwards the cockpit hood was pulled shut.

Although the November days were still hot, the nights were cold. I remembered my geography on how deserts formed through extreme variations of temperature — "large diurnal range." During three weeks in Boyce's unit we moved up through the Western Desert in the wake of the Eighth Army's final advance. We saw battle-weary divisions pull back towards the Nile Delta and fresh ones — New Zealanders, tough little Ghurkas, Scots and East Africans — roll forward to replace them. We became adept at striking camp as we moved west: Wadi Natrun, Sidi Haneish, Mersa Matruh, Derna, El Adem, Tobruk, El Ghazala — names etched with fire into British battle-history. We picked up a group of shocked soldiers freshly escaped from captivity. Forced to ride on their German captors' tanks to discourage our own from attacking, in the heat of an encounter they had jumped off into slit trenches. But they had been recaptured, to be imprisoned in a barbed-wire cage patrolled by Italian tanks; for the sport of it the Italians gunned them, killing or wounding many. Eventually the position was overrun by the Eighth Army and the survivors were slowly making their way towards the Delta. They were in bad shape. This was my first encounter, albeit vicarious, with the senseless brutality of war, and it enraged me.

Moving virtually every other day, we grew accustomed to sleeping in the open under the wings of our Hurricanes; to making do on half-a-gallon of water a day for washing, drinking, cooking and whatever else;

to a starvation diet of bullybeef and hard tack — large dog-biscuits into which you could only get your teeth because you were starving; to wearing our only clothes day and night, days on end, because there was insufficient water to wash them in; to limitless oceans of sand and dust which choked us; to baking sun by day and near frost at night. The Germans sent reconnaissance planes over several times a day, especially at first light. Early one morning the distant rattle of cannon fire signalled that Nipper Boyce had shot down a Junkers 88. We drove over in his jeep to inspect what was left of it, hot fragments of metal scattered in the burning sand. We came across a graveyard of German Air Force planes, strafed into uselessness where they stood on the perimeter of an abandoned desert strip. Scrambling down into sandbagged bunkers which a day earlier had been part of the enemy defences, we pocketed badges and medals of the dead Germans and Italians waiting for burial, and I hardly shuddered. It was the beginning of a madness which, paradoxically, was to preserve my sanity over the ensuing years. The episode landed me with fleas which remained intimate companions for several weeks.

The desert Bedouin were frequent visitors to the tents in which we had lived since leaving Khartoum, though now they were smaller than those at Almaza. They were no Rudolph Valentinos in flowing white robes and exotic headdresses, but dirty little men in old army jackets and baggy trousers, intent on barter. They produced German and Italian pistols, ammunition for them, and eggs, which we exchanged for tea and sugar.

There was a serious market for those commodities, of which the Cairo operators must have been unaware, otherwise the items would never have got as far as us. The price varied from day to day, sometimes hardening in our favour but mostly (as is usual with markets) it went against us, as guns and eggs became scarcer. At about eleven each morning, sitting in or around our tents drinking tea or coffee, we waited for the Bedouin.

"Salaam aleikum," they greeted us, with a disarming wave of the empty hand.

"Aleikum salaam. Ezzayak?" (How are you?)

"Hamdu l'Illah" (Praise God — meaning : I am well, thank God).

"Hamdu l'Illah," we repeated, then it was their turn until a score or more of alternating Hamdu l'Illahs had been enounced, only after which did good manners allow us to get down to the business in hand. None of us was in a hurry.

"Ekkis?" they enquired with an air of innocence, producing perhaps two tiny eggs from somewhere in the remoter regions of their baggy pantaloons, and fully aware of our hunger.

"Kam feloos?" we asked — (How much?)

"La, la, la, la, la!" with a reproachful finger wag — "mish feloos — shahi wa sukker." (Not money — tea and sugar.)

"Ashra ekkis, wahed kebaya sukker", we offered — one mugful of sugar for ten eggs, the enamelled services mug being a traditional measure throughout the desert. They were keen too on our flying-boots, wool-lined suede with wide necks to allow easy fitting over whatever trousers we wore, and zipped up the front. It was rumoured that their desperate poverty meant they couldn't marry and solaced themselves with their favourite ewes; and that their keenness for our boots was not so much to keep their feet warm as to anchor the hind legs of a ewe. The barter normally went on for the best part of an hour before they moved on to the next tent. Both sides enjoyed the contact.

My belly distended painfully and I was packed off to a field hospital outside Tobruk, a giant marquee with lines of empty beds awaiting field casualties, where my condition was diagnosed as chronic gastritis, doubtless brought on by uncomplicated apprehension. The only other inmates were two African soldiers in beds at the far end of the marquee, who quarrelled with each other ceaselessly. One of them resented the preferential treatment accorded to the other, who was being dosed with a larger pill; honour was satisfied by the administration of a really liberal dose of cascara. I was allowed up and walked in the sand by the Mediterranean, the bluest sea ever; I happened upon a tiny square of turf and marched round and round it.

Three days later I was back in Nipper Boyce's pool in time to move on to Martuba, Cyrene the Beautiful, and Barce, with each move appreciating the desert's differing faces. Pure sand near the Delta changed to stony dust at Tobruk near Barce the earth was sandy red with sprinklings of parched scrub below a long escarpment which ran parallel with the vivid sea. Rommel and his Afrika Korps were skeltering hell-for-leather through Tripolitania, and Montgomery's Desert Rats had to strain to keep up with them. Both the Army and Air Force were thinning out to garrison the route through the vacant desert, where lines of communication easily became extended. Thousands of prisoners poured back, the Italians unescorted and obviously delighted to be alive and out of the fighting, the Germans for the most part sullen and depressed; it was impossible not to admire men who had suffered the hardships of battle.

At that stage of my career, before the majority of us on the Operational Training Unit course in Scotland had carried out a single operational sortie, eleven were already dead, and another six had either failed to reach operational units or had been "grounded" for some reason or other. Being grounded was opprobrious — unless because of injury, it could only come about through abysmal failure, technical or moral; it was the severest of judgements. The dead were to a small extent the result of enemy action, in the case of the handful who had joined squadrons ahead of the rest, but all too frequently the deaths were accidental. There seemed to be almost daily news of Bob this, Bill that, Harry the other, who had "bought" it. Those of us who had so far survived were put on our mettle and somehow elevated into supermen whose existences were charmed. But it was not long before we realised, as pilot after pilot lost his life, that if a man continued to fly he would surely die, no matter how talented he was at his art.

Five of us were posted to No. 33 Squadron, to replace an equal number of deceased or retired pilots.

No. 33, a Hurricane squadron, had been part of the Desert Air Force and was now part of the garrison left at Benghasi, a peacetime Italian Airforce field, to protect that area of North Africa. A key harbour and communications centre, Benghasi was far and away the largest town in the desert. The airfield must have been de luxe before the war hit it; there were concrete mess-rooms and living quarters, a control tower, roads, water pipes, and all manner of civilised appendage. Not that any of them worked, after the successive batterings and counter-batterings of the preceding two years. But the earth was red and rich, and cool avenues of cypresses, pines and oaks sprouted here and there. No wonder the Italian settlers who had created the place had christened it "Benina."

The Squadron consisted of some two hundred and forty men, of whom twenty four were pilots; before we joined the strength had been down to nineteen. A fighter squadron aims to have a minimum of twelve aircraft available for a mission at any moment of time, so there were two pilots to each aircraft. In fact, due to the efficiency of the ground crews, there were often as many as fifteen or sixteen aircraft available, which meant that three or four were standbys; the remainder were either under repair, or having their guns or electrics serviced. After a specified number of hours flying, all of them had a thorough overhaul, however excellent their condition.

We five new boys were Englishmen, but apart from the Commanding Officer (a Battle of Britain pilot with a Distinguished Flying Cross) and two others, the

75

pilots were from everywhere else on the globe —
Australians, Americans, Canadians who called us
"Limeys", a New Zealander, who used wonderful
eighteenth-century expletives such as "'Od's hounds"
and "'Od's teeth"; and there was even a Dane. The
Australians called us "Pommies" or, more usually,
"Pommy bastards," the Canadian version of which was
"Goddam Poms," but it was in good humour. I felt very
much a new boy and out of my depth amongst that
tough, experienced bunch. Although during the nine
ensuing months I was not to encounter the opportunity
of dicovering the sterner stuff of which I might partly
be made, I was nevertheless at last truly "operational,"
and entitled to wear the fighter-pilot's scarf, a scrap of
discarded parachute silk which was considered lucky. In
the Mess we listened reverentially, and advantageously,
to the talk of the father-figures, some as much as three
years older than I. Sands, one of the Americans, kept
quiet about his age but was reputed to be as old as
twenty seven and had been flying since Pontius was
a . . .

Allotted to "A" Flight I came under the jurisdiction
of Allen James, a quiet good-natured Canadian to whom
I was to owe an important debt. Of slim, moderate
build, with blue eyes, he could have been a country
parson. His calm manner demanded a dog-collar rather
than a pilot's wings. His deputy Flight-commander was
Bill Fender, a tough Australian who found me puzzling,
and swung between rough intolerance and warm friendliness.
Basically he had a heart of gold, but having fought his
way through life to superb physical and mental toughness,

he knew no other way to communicate with his fellows. I knew I exasperated and worried him, sometimes to distraction. I flew as his Number Two, that is I flew my Hurricane immediately astern of him, "sitting on his tail", and followed like a little lamb, except that Number Twos were expected to protect not only their own rears but also their master's, the section leaders. It worked this way: an airborne fighter squadron of twelve aircraft was divided equally, for administrative as well as operational purposes, into "A" and "B" Flights. Each Flight was subdivided into three sections of two aircraft — in "A" Flight, Red, Yellow and White, in that order of priority; and in "B" Flight, Blue, Black and Green. Red One led Red section, with Red Two behind him, and so on. As Flight-Commander Red One normally led "A" Flight on occasions when six aircraft flew together, but when twelve aircraft were put up, it was under the leadership of the Squadron-Commander, either under the guise of Red One or Blue One. "B" Flight flying on its own would be led by its Flight-Commander, Blue One. There was considerable importance in the hierarchy, White Two and Green Two being the lowest form of life — naturally, the newest pilots — waiting for the day when they might be elevated to Yellow or Black Two respectively. In fact, 33 Squadron only put up twelve aircraft on two occasions during my stay with them, when we flew in what was called "battle formation".

Number Twos justified their existence by their ability to protect their Number Ones (whose mind might be occupied by loftier things), accomplished by the simple expedient of looking backwards as they flew frontwards.

In case that sounds difficult, it was! Although the Hurricane boasted a rear-view mirror, its use was strongly discouraged by the Number Ones. New boys had to learn quickly how to "weave", that is to fly behind their Number One (who would be flying straight and level) yet at the same time perform quick and regular turns to right and then left to enable them to look up their own backsides. The snaking movement led to various complications — one could lose formation, feel sick, get a crick in the neck, and roar one's engine to cover the extra mileage, which meant using a lot more petrol than the Number Ones and overheating into the bargain. I disliked the physical unpleasantness of heat, noise, vibration and neck-rack, and that is where Bill Fender's lesson came in. He must have known what it was like, as even the most experienced fighter pilot must sometime or other have flown as a Number Two, but he bawled down the radio at me, "Weave, you bastard!" when I was already weaving my very heart out. To be able to hear that agonising yell to this day means it must have been repeated frequently.

"Weave, Yellow Two! Weave, you bastard! Pull your bloody finger out!"

My poor Hurricane groaned with me as we skeltered sweatily along together, twisting and weaving behind that fiendish deputy Flight-Commander, our faces boiling and our fuel running short.

"Pour on the herbs, Yellow Two — open your bloody throttle!", when my bloody throttle had been wide open from the start, for Number Twos were naturally enough allocated the most clapped-out of the planes

The other exercise I loathed was formation aerobatics, again because one's inferior status meant flying the oldest of the Hurricanes and because of one's physical situation. Six of us in line astern, one behind the other, played at follow-my-leader. All very well for the leader, with a decent plane, and perhaps for the second and third men in the line. But as last man it was less fun. If the manoeuvre was a slow roll, rotating the aircraft round its own axis through three hundred and sixty degrees, there wasn't much to it except that sometimes I ended up a thousand or so feet below the others. But when a loop was involved it meant that whilst the last man was still diving the leader was halfway up and over, and you could see him above you. Moreover, the requisite amount of engine power increased as the end of the line was reached, the more power used the more "torque", or twist, was applied to the airframe, and the more difficult it was to control the aircraft.

The passage of a plane through the air creates a disturbance akin to the bow wave and the wake of a ship — slipstream. Hitting the turbulent slipstream of the aircraft in front is avoided by flying slightly below it, and the sixth man in a line astern formation is probably something like sixty feet below the leader. A simple calculation shows that the radius of a circle described by Number One is rather less than that of Number Six. Consequently, by the time old Tail-end Charlie approached the top of a loop his plane was in or approaching a state of stall, the result of which was to slide off and flick away into a spin, diving straight towards the unduly-familiar sight of a rapidly revolving, rapidly approaching earth. In those days of induction I was usually Number Six, and steadily grew familiar with the miseries of formation aerobatics. Jet aircraft do not suffer from engine torque or insufficiency of power, yet I have never seen a line astern loop essayed by as many as six jets. Not that our wartime standard of flying can be compared with the enormous proficiency and polish of the peacetime fighter pilots.

But if those moments were grim and perhaps almost miserable, they were compensated for by the occasions when on dawn patrol we were airborne at first light, and soon above the clouds we watched them slowly floodlit into spectacular salmon as the sun suffused and transformed them with a fairy-like irradiation. There was a wonderful calm and peace early in the morning, thirty thousand feet above the suffocating desert. It was on such occasions that for a fleeting moment everything that was inexplicable suddenly stood revealed in the clearest terms of understanding. Possessed of a magical insight into the unknown and incomprehensible, one was momentarily empowered to pass through the locked doors of secret worlds, a sensation lasting a tiny fraction of time — the rare intimation of mortality, immortality, universal comprehension, omniscience, which passed as swiftly as it had occurred. Perhaps occasional escape from flat reality hinted at the direction of a new dimension, a hidden window giving out on to infinity — or perhaps more simply it provided an acceptable explanation of why I was up there and what I was doing.

One day Allen James took me for a diplomatic walk, and in the kindliest fashion explained that unless one really loved flying one could never expect to be much good at it. I understood him — I knew that one cannot be excellent at anything unless one loved it. Much as I enjoyed squadron life, and liked the other pilots immensely, I knew also that it must still be some time ahead that my love of flying would grow sufficiently to bring me anywhere near the standard of the others. In fact it was not to be until a lot later.

Living conditions at Benina were tolerable because both our quarters and the Mess were decent buildings, rather than tents. Although they had been bashed about by the circumstances of war they still provided very much more comfort than camping out. The Mess was a large cool room, with a high ceiling, the whole washed white, and furnished meagrely. That did not matter, because here we met in the evenings and talked our way through until bedtime, to some extent about our pre-flying lives but predominantly about planes and the war. Food was sparse and poor, and I quickly lost nine kilos of my not very great weight. Water was in short supply, and we learnt to make the best use of what little there was — swilling it round the mouth to refresh the membranes before swallowing, rather than gulping it down, sipping minute drops rather than pouring it down the throat, however parched, and swallowing instead of spitting out the tiny amounts we allowed ourselves for dental hygiene. We pooled and saved up part of our ration until there was sufficient for a mighty laundry session in a communal oildrum blazing like a witches' cauldron over a fire which was made of petrol-soaked sand in another, smaller, oildrum. Then we spread the garments out to sear dry in a few minutes on the burning surface of the sand.

We had little to comfort us. Cigarettes were few, and of a special type reputedly manufactured locally out of dried camel-dung. They caught acridly at the throat, and we saved them for barter. Alcohol was virtually non-existent; out of an official ration of one pint of beer a fortnight, we received about half a bottle a month of strange Egyptian beer which was alleged to have close connections with the Suez Canal. We wondered where the rest of our rations went to, but only found out rather late about the uniformed profiteers based at Headquarters in Cairo and similarly comfortable pitches. Wounds took weeks to heal, and even the most innocent scratch turned into unpleasant, scabby desert sores, from which it was difficult to drive away the voracious, aggressive flies which attacked us non-stop. I became adept at fly-swatting, using only bare hands, and on one memorable occasion slayed no less than a hundred and twelve in an hour flat — I was aspiring to an average of two a minute. Somewhere there was a sign which told us that every time we killed a fly, eight hundred thousand died — what's that multiplied by a hundred and twelve?

The Germans regularly bombed us, always at night, occasionally destroying a few planes and killing some of us. We resented being their specific target and took to night-flying to try and knock them down, though we were not a night-fighter squadron. Climbing into the tiny cockpit in complete darkness was unpleasant. We strapped on the parachute already in place on the metal bucket-seat and the aircraft fitter stood on one wing, the rigger on the other, and helped us fasten the safety harness which held us to the seat. It was eerie going through the familiar cockpit drill, which included testing the controls and preparing to fire the giant engine. The manoeuvres were delicate and complex. At last you yelled "Contact!" and the batteries on the starter-trolley alongside the plane whined as the airscrew groaned and turned, then with a stutter and a roar the engine kicked into life, throwing terrifying flames and sparks from the multiple exhaust stacks along both sides of the engine cowling. By the dim light of a torch the ground crew signalled that they had pulled away the chocks from in front of the wheels, then you were alone in the night, taxiing much too fast to the flarepath and take-off point, with nothing visible whereby to gauge your speed. As the throttle was opened wide for take-off, flames and sparks shot alarmingly past each shoulder as though the entire contraption was about to ignite. Acceleration over the ground was bumpy, then less bumpy, then with a sudden lurch into the dark night sky you were airborne, the whole operation quite different from the smoothly controlled daylight take-off. An almost panicky jab at the lever which raised the undercarriage was succeeded by easing back the wide-open throttle, the pitch of the airscrew was varied from coarse towards fine, and only then did you address the cockpit instruments, lit by a stealthy side-glow.

It took every bit of ten minutes to settle down and feel easy, but by then the radio controller had issued directions of your course and altitude towards the night raiders, and you tore through the night sky towards the intruders whom you seldom spotted but whom the controller told you had been successfully chased away. When you did spot them they were always some thousands of feet above you and dived away home faster than you could fly the moment they spotted you below them. Returning to base was easy, the phosphorescence of the Mediterranean making it difficult to get lost as you descended towards the glimmer of the distant gas-fuelled flarepath, pulled down the lever which lowered the undercarriage, then the flaps which slowed you down and reduced the stalling speed, eased back the throttle, then fined the pitch of the airscrew, looking over your left side, the cockpit canopy back and your seat lowered, as the flares shot into line the stick was eased gently back and the throttle closed, waiting for the bump as the wheels touched earth, then the difficult job of keeping straight without any physical objects to focus on other than the flares, the sweating relief at being down safely, altogether a hit-and-miss affair. "Only fools and birds fly," we used to say, "and even birds don't fly at night."

On joining the Squadron we had been equipped with Smith and Wesson .38 revolvers with an effective range of about a metre, after which the bullets plummeted smartly groundwards. But through trade with the Bedouin we owned German Luger and Italian Beretta automatic pistols, beautiful and powerful weapons with which we became proficient. "Happy" Dettinger, one of our Canadians, showed infinite patience in teaching me how to handle a heavy automatic, and before long I could hit an empty can with the best of them. It was humbling that the tough outdoor Aussies and Cannucks showed such friendliness towards perhaps more soigné but certainly less tough and less outdoors-practical Limeys. There was an excellent rapport between us, and consequently the esprit-de-corps of the whole Squadron was unmistakeable. After all, we were living side by side under rugged conditions, far from our homes, daily risking our young necks in a common cause. We also shared a common dislike of the adjutant and the intelligence officer, both out of their depth among the outspoken, fit youths who regarded them as specimens of the wingless wonder. With the cruel self-centredness of youth we casually attached the label "penguin" to officers wearing Air Force uniform who did not fly, seldom pausing to consider whether there might not be some genuine physical or psychological insufficiency which prevented their doing so. Even had we considered, we would brusquely have brushed aside the theorem, peremptorily dismissing it as "bullshit." The songs of Lilli Marlene, even though full of bullshit and broadcast from Germany, were addressed to the fighting men and not to the penguins.

"Really, boys," she drawled, "do you think your wives and sweethearts will want you when you get back home with an arm or leg missing, or worse? — if you ever get back home! What do you think they are doing now, your wives and sweethearts, with all those Americans and Poles back in Britain taking your place?" There was also a strange pair of propagandists assailing us from an unidentified Central European station which we took to be Sofia. Their signature tune, sung in strange English, was "Africa Moon, Africa Stars." Unlike the glamorous, sexy Lilli Marlene they were ineffably dreary. Day after day they told us of the thousands of grosz rezhistered tons of Allied shipping which the Axis had sunk, without loss on their own side; they were too absurdly one-sided for belief, their propaganda failing through sheer exaggeration. We nevertheless enjoyed them, until they started telling whoppers about matters within our own knowledge, whereupon we became bored and switched them off.

"Bullshit" was a word of criticism frequently directed against the only one of the pilots who was a real outsider, poor Windrush, who insisted he was from San Francisco. Although he had an American-style accent, his features and pigmentation pointed unmistakeably to the Anglo-Indian half-castes I was to encounter later, and our Americans and Canadians embarrassed him cruelly. Why worry whether he was a Yank or a Chink, a Frog or a Wog, a Yid, or anything but a Hun, Wop or Nip, the hated foes. He had to eat, excrete, sleep, sweat, copulate like the rest of us. If only copulation were a reality instead of a distant dream . . . He and his plane disappeared soundlessly into the sea one day and all that was left was to send his things to a San Francisco address where the name was not Windrush; some distant uncle, it turned out, from the sad acknowledgement that came back.

Pilots departed regularly and new ones arrived to take their place, but gradually the international complexion of the Squadron disappeared. Before each departure there was a farewell party, whether the pilot was departing or departed. One such party led to a minor war. Outside the Mess building a tall wireless-mast was surmounted by a circular platform, fifty feet up and approached by an iron-runged ladder. At the time the Germans were imitating the British Long Range Desert Groups, parties of highly-trained men of great courage who operated far behind the enemy lines to destroy men and machines in surprise raids. The guards around our airfield were in consequence slightly trigger-happy, very much on the alert, for they would be the first target.

Phil Lambert, a delightful Australian on excellent terms with the world, was leaving us. After his farewell party had been in progress a couple of hours he felt the need to fulfil a longstanding ambition by climbing up to the circular platform. Anxiously we watched his slightly alcoholic ascent, but once he had arrived we returned to the business in hand. A little later, Drain Prentice, so called because of his frequent visits to the wooden latrines standing shamelessly in the open sand, selected the foot of the mast to relieve himself. He was a massively-built Australian blond with a wonderfully good nature, who withstood any amount of leg-pulling. His reply to comments on his outsize backside was

"Well, yer carn't drive a ten-inch nail with an eight-ounce 'ammer!" Unfortunately he chose the precise moment as Lambert, still aloft, felt the same need. There was a mighty yell of wrath from the drenched Drain who pulled out his revolver and opened fire at the platform where Phil, ignorant of why he was being attacked and by whom, returned fire vigorously as we all rushed from the building with guns drawn, believing the Germans must have sneaked a L R D G into the camp. The guards at the gate opened fire at the mast, convinced too that the Germans were there, and the two Aussies returned their fire, one from atop the mast and the other from its foot. Realising what had happened, we rushed a messenger round to the guardroom to effect a truce, and eventually peace was restored without anybody having been hurt — except the damp and sulky Drain.

The desert, rather than the unnatural way of life towards which we had to adjust, accentuated our individual peculiarities. There was so little available — little food, and that as bad as campaign rations can be, predominantly the molten bully-beef and so-called biscuits — no comforts beyond the shared radio, no entertainment, no women, no shops, no houses, no mail from home, just our little band obliged to provide everything for ourselves and each other in our efforts to stay sane. Just our little band, and sand, and fierce flies. Individualism manifested itself in our clothes — hats crumpled and crushed out of recognisable shape, khaki drill of variegated colours and styles, footwear exceedingly irregular. Burnt brown by the hot African sun, we were lean through insufficient food, sinewy from our occupation. We were "sand-happy", desert-happy, "shwyea magnoon" (Arabic for "slightly mad") — we had a host of adjectives to describe each other's condition, the amalgam of boredom, homesickness, sex-starvation, war-weariness, hunger and despair, which comprised an imbalance which was indeed close to insanity. Yet there was a strong admixture of confidence and youthful hope, and the pride of belonging to a polished fighting unit. As well as shooting practice we thought up weird entertainments. At night, sallying forth in jeeps, we hunted desert foxes, fixing their brushes to our windscreens — callous sport, though doubtless appreciated by the Senussi shepherds. We read whatever books we could get our hands on, seated in the sun on the "thunder-boxes", the open-air latrines set here and there in pairs, which led to my being constipated for two weeks until I acquired the necessary disinhibition. We wrote innumerable letters home, and the fortnightly mail plane brought an occasional reply for the lucky ones — later I discovered that perhaps one letter in ten sent from home reached us out there.

Two squadrons, of which we were not one, were sent on a crazy raid on Crete, across two hundred miles of ocean from Derna, not far along the road. With long-range tanks the Hurricanes managed about a hundred and fifty miles an hour, and had enough fuel to make the round trip. But at that speed they were sitting ducks for the German anti-aircraft gunners. Not one plane got back. The gentleman who dreamed that one up had done it before, when he had sent a Hurricane wing to attack the island of Cos, off the Turkish coast; he was known as "the Wizard of Cos". But we were warriors trained to execute without question the commands of our superiors.

We too flew out over the sea, but at that period it was to practise gunnery, using the white-capped waves as our targets. They were a useful target because, like an airplane, they didn't stay still — one had to wait for them to form, then immediately fire, the bezel at the top of the joystick previously swivelled to the red danger "Fire" position and the illuminated head-up gunsight switched on.

Two months after my joining 33 Squadron we moved out of Benina to make room for a Wing of United States Air Force Liberator bombers, who commenced attacking what Churchill described as "the soft underbelly of Europe" — Italy, and the Romanian oilfields. There was an enormous gulf between American and British standards of troop comfort — they were better dressed, better housed, better entertained. But they were a fighting unit and we admired them — there is something in common between all fighting men, the five per cent of the armed forces who stick their necks out, something much stronger than the relationship between them and the headquarters opportunists, over-concerned to preserve the integrity of their skins, and who engendered in us a rather violent prejudice which acted as a fillip to the sustaining of our hardships.

We were not pleased at having to quit our cosy billet, but set up a tented camp at Bersis, along the coast, resuming our matutinal relations with the Bedouin, barred from Benina's snazzy precincts. At eleven each morning the air became heady with the aroma of coffee cooked up in a petrol-tin upon a fire consisting of another petrol-tin filled with sand into which petrol was poured liberally then ignited. Petrol was one commodity of which there was no shortage. To some extent due to our protective/defensive existence, the supply fleets which had for long been denied passage through the Mediterranean were now once again plying. My coffee brew, laced with disgusting thick sweet condensed milk, according to my Special Desert Recipe, attracted the shabby little desert shepherds who shyly approached, and the bargaining began. Their eggs became increasingly small, and as the war moved further and further away from us the market hardened, so that in no time a Luger or Beretta automatic pistol was costing a couple of hundred cigarettes Wa an old shirt, Wa ten kebayas of sukker, Wa ... Trade was bad, but we continued to refuse to part with our flying-boots. Perhaps they were put off by our sleeping-bags strewn along the sloping tent walls inside out, for the sun to flush out the undauntable fleas which tormented us. Or perhaps they were embarrassed at our improvised chattis (clay water-jugs), which were our kitbags, filled with water and suspended in the direct sun from the tent guy-ropes; the porosity of the kitbags enabled evaporation, with consequent cooling of the water in the bag. Water was now plentiful, tankers plying the lines of tents twice daily.

Hour after long hour we sat at daily readiness awaiting the call to action, four pilots (two sections) in a tent alongside the runway where the Hurricanes stood, and connected by a field telephone to the Army radar unit just up the road. Whenever we heard aircraft engines we scanned the dazzling African skies. "If yer caren't see 'em when you hear 'em," growled Fender, "how the f — d'you expect to see 'em when yer caren't!" Whiling away the hours in the folding canvas camp chairs was an exercise at which we became expert — talking, reading, playing cards, drinking the sickly tea constantly brewed by the Operations Clerk, a bookie's clerk in civilian life and brimful of cockney humour. We were on for four hours at a stretch, time enough to dismember and reassemble one's revolver — I always had a dozen or so bits left over. As well as the Smith & Wesson .38, we were armed with a silk map, a tiny pocket compass, a purse of silver coins and a "ghoolie-chit", the last two in case of being forced to land in the desert whose inhabitants were not always as amiable as our local friends. The "ghoolie-chit", in English and Arabic, informed the reader that the bearer was a British flying officer and a friend of all Arabs, who if taken alive and unharmed to the nearest British military post would be exchanged for a substantial sum of money. The purse of silver, worth £50, was considered to be an adequate down-payment. The chit was a much cherished possession of every pilot. Word had it that unhappy captives had been known to have their testicles removed and stitched into their mouths; or the victim might be buried in sand with only the head left sticking out, smeared with honey alongside an anthill. At an early stage I committed to memory a phoneticisation of the Arabic words, in case my captor couldn't read.

Slouched in khaki shirts and shorts, with our fur-lined flying-boots, and girt around by voluminous lifejackets known as "Mae Wests", after a well-endowed Hollywood actress of the time, we awaited the tense moment when the field telephone rang and the bookie's clerk foamed at the corners of his mouth, his eyes popping out on long stalks, and we were off and away before he could even start yelling "S C R A M B L E!". As we raced to the Hurricane wingtips where our parachutes with their inflatable dinghy seats were perched, snatching at the dangling straps to buckle on the 'chute, he fired a vivid red cartridge from a Very pistol. At the same time, the fitter and rigger assigned to each plane rushed to help our wild preparations.

Almost before the 'chute-cum-dinghy had walloped our buttocks we had climbed on to the wing and into the cockpit, and while the ground crew draped the safety harness across one's body the be-goggled helmet was snatched from its perch on the control column, then the safety harness slickly pinned through. Ignition switches on, the seat lowered, the hydraulics checked, "Rich" fuel mixture selected, the propeller lever slammed forward to Fine Pitch, throttle lever a quarter open, fuel to "On", flaps selected to "Up", carburetters primed, "Contact!" yelled to the ground crew squatting at the starter-trolley. The engine fired, the crew pulled away the wheel chocks, the throttle was opened fully, then the aircraft rolled away bumping along the ground, accelerating swiftly but smoothly; as the tailplane lifted the plane's nose was held down by trimming the elevator control gently forward, wheels selected Up, throttle now wide open for maximum revs to climb into the brilliant sky in a battle climb of five thousand feet a minute with the engine roaring its heart out. From the phone's ring to being airborne has taken under two minutes. Radio switched on, microphone-cum-oxygen-mask clipped across, IFF (Identification Friend or Foe) radar gadget which transmits a signal to the scanning radar screens flicked on.

"Hello Hellfire, Gluebox Red section airborne. Red One, cockerel crowing" (IFF switched on). "Hellfire, Red Two, cockerel crowing" . . . and so on.

"Gluebox Leader, this is Hellfire, bogey (unidentified aircraft) at angels thirty-five (thirty-five thousand feet), vector two six zero" (steer a course of 260 degrees).

"Hellfire, Gluebox Leader, willco" (will cooperate).

And away we went, climbing flat out into the clear desert sky. We turn on the oxygen bottle control cock; without the oxygen we would become tipsy at fifteen thousand feet, blind drunk at twenty-five thousand, and plummet to earth stupefied at thirty thousand. The oxygen was moist and cool, the noise as we suck it in amplified through the radio. Sweet comfort of living. As we ascended to do battle the Number Two's weaved like mad, eyes rolling round the heavens to spot the enemy. At twenty thousand feet Hellfire's voice comes through: "Gluebox Leader, bandit (identified enemy aircraft) now at angels thirty-seven, vector two-seven-fo-er."

"Hellfire, this is Gluebox Leader, roger (message received and understood), willco."

At thirty-two thousand feet Hellfire would give a fresh change of course and tell us the bandit was now at angels forty. The cold was intense. Teeth chattered and knees knocked, partly through cold, partly excitement, partly fear. We gasped in loud gulps of oxygen. We knew the bandit must be a reconnaissance plane, probably a specially modified Junkers 52. There were his vapour trails above us, but the Hurricanes were now hardly climbing. Ahead there was only dust haze. We staggered to thirty-five thousand feet, but the controls were sloppy and unresponsive. We got to thirty-six thousand, and Jerry was grinning down at us.

"Hellfire calling Gluebox Leader, bandit is at angels forty-two." We know he was. We are at our ceiling height and could only hope he was stupid enough to come down, as we drifted helplessly under him. In frustration I pulled my nose up and fire a useless burst at him, which causes the Hurricane to stall. Jerry's vapour trail curved as he turns away northwards and out over the Mediterranean to Crete, which was his base. At least we had frightened him off. I was rigid with cold.

"Gluebox Leader, this is Hellfire; bandit is going home. You may pancake (land)." Leader waggled his wings, half-rolled over on to his back, pulled the stick hard back into his stomach and screamed earthwards.

The other three Hurricanes followed suit and within a couple of minutes were pitched back into the desert's blazing heat over Bersis, easing back out of the suicidal dive, and suddenly it was warm and comfortable and secure. The speedometer needle slurs back erratically from three hundred and forty to a hundred miles an hour, then the landing drill — wheels down, fine pitch, fuel on to gravity tank, mixture rich, flaps down and a moment later we had landed, taxied in and switched off. I would sit for minutes, exhausted by the over-expenditure of adrenalin, and before I had started to climb out the aircraft was being refuelled from the great bowser tankers. Back at the tent we reported to the Operations Officer and drank the clerk's nauseating tea to thaw out. The sweat on my feet has frozen and it was half-an-hour before my flying-boots unstuck from them and I could pull them off.

Scrambles were mostly of that sort, though ocasionally the bandits would be a couple of intrusive Junkers 88 light bombers which we chased back out to sea, unable to catch them in our clapped-out old Hurricanes. At least, they never dropped a single bomb, but if only we had Spitfires. The heart-pounding of each scramble must have knocked a few months off our young lives, but they served their purpose, at the same time demonstrating our complex technical skills and encouraging the dedicated ground crews.

When not at Readiness we flew defensive patrols, either tearing hopefully up and down the desert in search of an elusive enemy, or policing the convoys by now more confidently ploughing the Mediterranean, still a dangerous occupation. They had to be approached with caution — from a predetermined direction, waggling your wings — not too little, not too much — you had to fire what were known as the "Colours of the Day" from a Very pistol (woe betide you if the Armoury Section had given you the wrong cartridge and you fired off the wrong colour), then flick on your radio. An inordinate quantity of crackle would be succeeded by a cultured voice inviting you to identify yourself. Each day we had a new password, and heaven help you if you got confused and gave yesterday's — all would be lost, for those cultured voices knew not mercy nor forgiveness, and ever since the Sunderland off West Africa, one was conscious of their beastly six-inch guns following one around the sky. Even after having escorted them for an hour or two it was foolhardy in the extreme to consider oneself safe, as one of our misguided young Aussie pilots discovered when, out of boredom, he dived down jocularly to beat up one of the convoys and was promptly shot down. Being cultured, they of course heaved him out of the sea.

There were two Sections on each patrol, one between five and ten thousand feet, and the other at five hundred. I did not enjoy the low level stooge, out of sight of land, and with only a single, increasingly sick-sounding engine to keep you in the air. The further one was from land the more the engine coughed and wheezed, but I only saw one fail, when another of our Aussies baled out at two hundred feet, his parachute opening exactly as his feet touched the water. He too fell a victim to culture, because the Navy took him on to Tripoli. For many of our patrols the Hurricanes were festooned with long-range tanks, torpedo-shaped containers slung beneath the wings, which enabled us to stay airborne for four hours. One hour of sitting on the inflexible dinghy attached to the parachute, which provided our seat, was enough for our lean backsides, and the agonies of shifting from one skinny buttock to the other in the tiny cockpit were infinite. A four-hour stint also created other problems, for which the Hurricanes provided no equipment, and it was with no small relief that we welcomed the next section of dots appearing on the horizon from the direction of Bersis, so that we could turn towards them and home.

On one such occasion we had hardly turned away from the convoy when the Navy opened up with its artillery, and the Hurricanes piled into a gang of Jerries which had been craftily awaiting our departure. It was very late in the afternoon, and they had decided we were the last patrol of the day. Five Heinkel 111s and Junkers 88s were shot down into the sea. Dunlop's Hurricane, hit by their counter-fire, span out of control as he floated down at the end of his silken canopy, to start swimming home. He became a member of "the Caterpillar Club" — aircrew who had succesfully baled out. But incidents like that were rare — the presence of the Hurricanes was a sufficient deterrent from enemy attack.

We became increasingly adept at making life less intolerable. Short rations and hard living turned us to all manner of escapist practice. We collected tortoises, on which we painted bright yellow identification marks, piling them up into towers with the biggest at the bottom and the babies at the peak. We ringed scorpions with petrol fire to watch them sting themselves to death (as legend had it) but they never obliged. We placed them face to face, when they were supposed to fight each other, but ours lacked the necesary instinct. We shot dice, exchanged life histories, swam in the sea close to a wrecked tanker, where the water was as warm as the naked brown bodies plunging into that incredible blueness, but for all that we were frequently bored beyond distraction into our special lunacy. At times we became sullen and morose, quarrelsome and despondent, lifeless and tetchy. "Nil nisi bastardium Britannicum carborundum," counselled one of our classically-minded Aussies — "Don't let the Pommie bastards grind yer down," but the mood of impotent anger was directed at "them", the faceless indeterminates who left us drifting hopelessly, directionless. Some superficial orientation would have satisfied us — a few more German planes daily, perhaps. We were frustrated, powerless to direct our own fates, even minimally. Had we had the sense to dig large holes in the sand we could have at least retired to our tents to fall asleep satisfied as we reflected on our creative labour, and with the prospect of filling them in again to look forward to. That was it — there was nothing to look forward to except more sand and flies, more appalling diet, more sex-starvation, and an hour or two's flying on what were all too often routine patrols.

As there were no spades we took to digging in the sands of our minds, mostly in private but occasionally at a "Brains Trust" organised by the donnish bent-backed orderly-room clerk, who strode about humming snatches of Prokofiev and quietly quoting Dostoievsky to himself. Reality was unpleasant and escape impossible. There were enough of us to prevent minds turning too far inwards, though in fact one or two broke under the strain and went off their rockers, to be repatriated, though the strains of desert life may only have been their final straw. We ceased to think of England as a place we had ever known, and now the infrequent letters that filtered through were received with indifference. We knew as well as "Lilli Marlene" what was going on in that country stuffed with so-necessary females, and of the droves of Yanks, Poles, Czechs, Norwegians, Free Frenchmen, Danes, Dutchmen, as well as home-based natives, there to please and enjoy them. It was cruel. A sense of frustrated bitterness harrowed us more frequently there in the endless sand mirroring a glittering sun, and shimmering with a doubled intensity of reflected heat.

CHAPTER
FIVE

Desert

But we were young, and when after some months Taffy Edwards and I were given a pair of Hurricanes to fly to Alexandria for repairs which could not be effected at Bersis, we rejoiced at the prospect of a change of scenery. The next day we left Alexandria on our way back home, carrying our parachutes and flying-helmets with their attached goggles and RT/oxygen mask. The awfulness of the women in the brothel we had visited had utterly dissolved my lust; I had waited in a corridor until Taffy emerged.

Slowly we hitched lifts in military vehicles down the black tarmac road spanning the hundred and fifty miles between Alex and Cairo, calling one by one at the airfields along its side to cadge a flight back to Benghasi. Luckless, we arrived in Cairo, complete with parachutes and helmets, looking and feeling ridiculous. As well as with headquarters johnnies, Cairo was stiff with civilians serving their country in educational and propaganda activities, which could be carried out in greater comfort than at home, where the towns and cities were being flattened by enemy bombing. It was a predominantly safe, unwarlike billet from which you could move out in good time were the enemy to look like breaking down the gate; the climate was lovely, and the relaxed facilities of the Gezira Club and racecourse were available within easy walking distance, along with golf, tennis and other civilised distractions. Not for them greasy bully-beef and hard tack, nor the half-gallon of water for combined bathing, cooking, drinking and laundry. Every campaign needs the backup of a host of uniformed non-combatants — the headquarters personnel concerned with policy, planning, personnel and so on — and of them too Cairo suffered no shortage. The extent to which their efforts contributed positively or negatively to the campaign's progress will always be a subject for fruitful discussion; the bitterness towards them inculcated in the fighting-men was a compound of disdain with a trace of envy. It was unfair twice over — the cost of their comfortable way of life might well have been directed to providing comfort for the fighting-men, and the pittance spent on the latter was more than adequate for those living sheltered lives. In company with the expatriate career educationists, the "Whitehall warriors", as they were universally known, ate cream-cakes in Groppi's, took pre-prandials on the terrace at Shepheard's Hotel overlooking the serene Nile, tiffin in the restaurant there, following which a nap would be appropriate before a round of golf at Gezira, ahead of cocktails at the Officers' Club, and then there was still the evening meal to be tackled. They also served who only sat and wasted — wasted time and money and often lives. But then, as every civil servant worthy of the name knows, the bother about decision-taking which involves others is that you may make a mistake and get into trouble, whereas by confining decision-taking strictly to your own personal position there is every chance of protecting and enhancing it.

At Heliopolis, Leon was eager to know about desert conditions. Cesare said, "C'est vrai? c'est vrai!" in horror at our mild tale, while Michelle in her frustration wailed continuously "Ya-ani, ya-ani?" I supposed that our life crammed in small tents, inadequately fed and watered, no consolatory cigarettes or alcohol to speak of, sleeping on campbeds with mosquitoes and fleas as bedfellows, fly-ridden, with sand in our eyes, food, hair and everywhere else, no cinemas, baths, shops, houses, flying hot uncomfortable planes in pursuit of hostile intruders, scorched by day yet at night cold, being bombed, low-level patrols far out over the inhospitable Mediterranean on a single rough engine, and the misery of daytime and nocturnal interceptions of an enemy almost always out of reach, the suffocation of emotions and consequent mental disturbance — all those must have sounded unattractive to those elegant metropolitan apartment-dwellers. My appearance, lean and brown, considerably thinner because nine kilograms lighter than my normal weight, alarmed them. There was no pleasure in recounting our way of life, lost as we were somewhere within an endless war, with no chance of escaping from it and yet rarely in the heart of it, while our youthful years poured wastefully away into the burning sands, and our comrades died one by one, far from home. Cairo seemed foul, stuffy and indecent, degraded and phoney as a city can be, and at Air Headquarters, Middle East, we solicited help in making a speedy return to the Squadron. Despite everything we hankered to be back in the desert with our comrades, back in the hopeless existence to which we belonged and which, being the way of life to which we had become accustomed, spelt security, where Cairo frightened and disgusted us.

At AHQ we ran into clean starched khaki men with clean starched khaki attitudes and voices, into petty mouths avid for tea and cream-buns . . . Cream-buns! We could not believe our eyes when the bold warriors stopped for their tea-break and the cream spurted between their teeth. Hungry in every possible way, a resentment crept into my soul at the sheer injustice of it and was to remain for a long time to come.

Although a transport plane visited Benghasi twice weekly, they could not sanction the carriage of passengers. Against Regulations. "But we have to get back to our Squadron!" — "Sorry. That's how it is." "Bloody bastards!" I breathed. We could easily have been squeezed aboard without fuss. It was not so much the exercise of their power of refusal as the arrogance of their attitude towards us. Yet, however unintentionally, that was what assisted in welding the fliers into a superficially lax but basically fierce brotherhood in arms. We absorbed a quantity of consolatory beer in a nearby bar; as happens on such occasions we fell into odd company, including some American flying men. "You boys wanna get your asses to Air Headquarters," they advised, and sure enough at AHQ, United States Army Air Force, Middle East, a jolly major said, "Sure, boys, take this to Heliopolis airfield and I guess they'll be able to fix you up." At Heliopolis we showed his bit of paper to another Yank major who said, "You see that Liberator at the end of the runway? — he's going to Benghasi. Just you run and you'll catch him." We ran, parachutes, helmets and all, exhilarated and sweating, waving frantic signals at the Liberator running up its engines at the end of the runway. We were seen. Its belly slid open and a smooth sergeant emerged, shouting above the engine-roar, "What's the trouble, boys?"

"Lift to Benghasi?" we screamed.

"Sure," he yelled, "climb in", so we climbed, the bomb-bay doors rolled shut and we followed him up the fuselage to the cockpit, bulging with thick carpet and luxuriuous wall-padding, then we were immediately off into the burning air and were on our way home to that which was familiar. How different from AHQ, Royal Air Force, Middle East!

Their ideas about navigation also differed from ours. While we drank coffee and shot dice with them, the automatic pilot coped with the Liberator, while the navigator played with a Course-and-Speed Calculator, a simple device we had used to work out elementary navigation during our training days, but not much use on a long trip, and a strange choice in a plane stuffed with elaborate electronic aids. At hourly intervals he announced our Estimated Time of Arrival, but once that had come and long since gone and we were still over the desert he began to look worried.

"ETA 1615," he said.

At 1630, "ETA 1715," he said.

At 1720, "ETA 1750," he said, then, "Say, you boys know this part of the world?"

I looked out.

"We've about an hour of daylight left. Alter course 15 degrees to starboard."

It was obvious that we were somewhere down in the desert, well out of sight of the coast, and at those latitudes night falls like a stone. Quarter-of-an-hour later we made another course change to starboard, then another, then yet another, until I recognised the Barce escarpment, a long red ridge of high ground running parallel with the coast.

"Alter course seventy degrees to port and you'll be spot on Benina airfield."

We arrived two hours later than the estimated time, in the dark. We must have been some three hundred miles south of our correct course. I was to have similar experiences of American air navigation later, but beyond doubt they were the kindliest and most relaxed and hospitable people. The Liberator was one of seventy or so that took off from Benina every morning to bomb the Axis oilfields at Ploesti in Romania. Never as many as seventy returned, and of those that did a fair number were always in a bad way, with one, two, or even three of their engines out of commission. We

106

admired the Americans, and used to cheer as their ragged formations approached home.

If the Liberator cockpit was the height of luxury, our Hurricanes represented the depth of utility. A scooped-out metal seat into which the strapped-on parachute-cum-dinghy fitted snugly; a dashboard with a multitude of dials and gauges, over which a quickly-acquired mastery enabled confident supervision with only intermittent glances; artificial horizon, rate-of-climb and rate-of-turn indicators, altimeter, oil pressure and engine temperature gauges, rev counter, clock, boost gauge; on the left-hand side of the cockpit the propeller pitch and fuel-mixture controls and throttle, on the top of which was a bomb-release button; below, the radio with press-button switches and a flick Transmit/Receive lever, and on the floor oxygen-bottles and knobs of various kinds, including controls for "trimming" the elevators and ailerons. On the right-hand side the quadrant and lever operating the undercarriage and wing-flaps, each selected either to Up or Down, and round the corner on the right the IFF — "Identification Friend or Foe" — the radar device codenamed the "cockerel." The control column came up between the pilot's knees with a bakelite loop to grip, and a large bevelled button top front which swivelled to allow the four twenty-millimetre cannon to be fired. Immediately in front of the pilot were the compass and a gyro-gunsight which threw a lighted image on to the windscreen, enabling him to fire with considerable accuracy. All of it bare metal, burning in the sun's heat, or blisteringly cold at high altitude, and always vibrating and roaring a rowdy fatigue through your whole being.

Our logbooks, most precious of our few possessions, were ruled in columns allowing for the identity of both first and second pilots — multi-engined pilots, where two shared the flying responsibilities, had the same logbook. It was our practice to enter our names as "Second Pilot", the space for "First Pilot" either being left blank, or simply marked "J.C."

A khamseen hit us, a scorching arid wind of storm force blowing from the bowels of the desert, lifting in its path a wall of sand hundreds of feet high, so that daylight was blotted out for three entire days, during which we lay gasping for air on our camp-beds, suffocating in stinging sand. Every surface was smothered in a layer of sand, and visibility was no more than the hand held in front of one's face. Once a day we found our way to the Mess tent for a tin of fruit or bully beef by crawling on hands and knees and clutching at the field-telephone wires strewn out in the sand, without which we would have been utterly lost. The temperature was a hundred and twenty-six, and had we not been young and fit not all of us would have survived. At the end of three days the blistering wind suddenly relented; red-eyed we staggered into the open where the sky was visible at last, patterned all over with mackerel scales at incredible altitude, and by that sign we knew that a rainstorm was coming which would wash away the sand piled up around our tents. Yelling with excitement, we moved towards the sea, the air soft and wet with accumulated moisture. As we raced into the ocean the heavens opened up and it rained for hours, plastering a thick mud skin on to the desert's surface, but we were revived.

From time to time we searched for missing boats, or bodies, or unwelcome submarines, flying in spread line abreast in search formation fifty feet above the waves, far out of sight of land, with only a solitary rough-running engine to preserve us from a watery end. It was comfortless. Happily, the Merlin engines were ruggedly reliable, for we alone would have been responsible had one failed — before take-off the pilot was obliged to sign a form acknowledging that he had fully examined his plane and its guts and was satisfied that it was eminently serviceable for the purpose for which it was provided. That really was rather a joke, especially if you were rushed into a sudden trip — there was no time to examine anything, except that it was an airplane and not a Number Eleven bus.

" 'Ere, mate," the Chiefy would say, "what d'yer fink this is — Fred Karno's bloody Circus? If the engine packs up you'd better put out your skyhooks!" How amazed they must have been only twenty years later to see the vertical take-off plane do just that. However, we were allowed, even encouraged, to report any defects after landing, which would perhaps be small consolation if the defect had landed you in the drink (ocean) or even in the desert, let alone the hereafter. One of our more cheerful songs had as its chorus, "No hope at all, no hope at all, If your engine packs up you'll have no hope at all!"

As well as the seductive ladies from Berlin and other points east we listened regularly to the BBC's news broadcasts and some of the apalling entertainment pushed out for our especial delight. If those dessicated females with their desexed voices announcing programmes of musical comfort could have heard the way they were received they would have chucked the job hurriedly. But our attitude was tainted by a growing bitterness at our general conditions, which seemed to go on and on without any improvement whatever.

A batch of new boys arrived all pink from Blighty and at last there was leave for the older residents. We went off at intervals in batches of four to seek the fleshpots of Cairo for a week. By now one of the senior pilots, my turn came round quickly. I picked up a Hurricane II D, the Tankbuster — armed with two forty-millimetre cannon whose shells could pierce the skin of a medium Hun tank — which had to be flight-tested and gun-tested before delivery to the Delta. Before firing the guns, the Tankbuster had to be put into a screaming dive, else the recoil would cause the plane to stall, and that could be fatal. As I pressed the gun-button I screwed up my eyes waiting for a mighty explosion, but there was just a dull "Thunk", the Hurricane halted in mid-air for a moment or so, then gathered momentum to resume flight. The others in the leave batch were an Aussie, Jack Cook, and a Dubliner, Paddy Avison. The Southern Irish had proved themselves mostly pro-German but those who

110

weren't were just as positively pro-British. Paddy was a charmer to the hilt, but unfortunately his charm failed and he went the way of all flesh shortly after that interlude, when he walloped a field-gun with his wing-tip during a beat-up, and that was the end of him, apart from the scrapings. He had at least enjoyed his leave; that was how we saw it.

Following the coastal road, a thick black ribbon of tarmac edged on one side with the brilliant blue of the Mediterranean and on the other with the tawny desert, we flew at a thousand feet, swooping down every now and then to investigate or beat up objects of interest, our innocent pleasure exemplifying our skill. From one such swoop Jack Cook failed to rise, as his Hurricane lost itself in the cloud of sand kicked up where its belly had scraped when his engine had failed. His charm had not, and as we orbited he climbed safely out and waved, we pinpointed his position then flew off to Mersa Matruh, a few miles away, to report the prang and to leave a message that we would rendezvous with him in Cairo.

Next day we hopped aboard the night train for Palestine which left Cairo at six each evening, to arrive at Rehovoth, a few miles outside Tel Aviv, at the same time the following morning. It was common knowledge in the desert that T. A. was a good leave spot, if quieter and less dynamic than Cairo. Just before dawn I peered out of the stationary sleeping-carriage window into a strange world girded in mist. The damp air was laden with orange blossom, most exquisite of perfumes, and through the mist in the slow white dawning there were trees — trees in every direction as far as the eye could see, and the first I had seen in a year. I had not realised how much I had missed them. I woke the others.

"Bloody trees!" I yelled. "Just sniff that perfume; it must be orange blossom."

Headily we climbed down from the immobile train where it stood in the middle of a vast orange grove just outside Rehovoth station, and swayed under the superlative intoxication of mist, trees and perfume. Half an hour later the train decanted us into the station, where we took a taxi the few miles into Tel Aviv, to laze our first days on the miniscule beach, to buy glasses of fresh-crushed orange juice at a penny a time. At a kibbutz, one of the communal settlements run along non-political and therefore tolerably accurate communistic principles, we were split up among several families and shown great hospitality as well as kindness. As souvenirs I gave their children precious baubles acquired in the desert, in particular a medallion inscribed on each side with hieroglyphics, and mounted on an axle attached to a lucky horseshoe so that the medallion could be flicked and spun; the hieroglyphics thereupon sorted themselves out into "VIVA BENGASI ITALIANA." The kibbutz hummed with well-directed activity and one remembered that those were pioneers carving a home out of wasteland. The bus back to Tel Aviv took us through a pretty village which I earmarked as a suitable hideaway — one of the funkholes one never stops seeking as a place of refuge, sanctuary and retreat from reality.

112

Tel Aviv was a manifestly half-developed town, where blocky raw concrete buildings adjoined sandy vacant lots and many of the roads were unmade, but a theatre, concert-hall, art galleries, bookshops and all the accessories of a cultured society were cosseted behind trees lining the main avenues. The Mediterranean and its breezes made it a perfect holiday pitch, and if the tiny beach was a bit crowded, that did increase the togetherness in which we found ourselves not altogether uninterested; the miniature beach was like an antheap and as well as warm swimming there was much to occupy our attention. Not all the Jews were opposed to Hitler and his regime, as I found when conversing with a highly intelligent watchmaker whose pretty daughter had attracted me into his shop. For some extraordinary reason, what had been an interesting conversation about inferiority complexes ended in a standing row.

"Wait till Hitler pushes you out of Egypt!" he roared at me. "He'll conquer the English and the whole of the Middle East."

Being kicked out of Germany by the Nazis had in no way impaired his loyalty to or admiration of his homeland. I found a doubt creeping into my mind.

A thin little Jewess of eighteen, with a wan haunted face, took me to a crummy hotel in Jaffa, the old Arab town adjoining T. A., a terrifying place round the corner where the coast hooked back in a hairpin bend, so that the town hall stood tall on a promontory sticking out into the Mediterranean. In the middle of the night someone tried the door of the room and I was put off the adventure. Then they tried the window; fortunately it was stoutly barred with iron. No love or sleep that night. In the morning the girl told me to go back to T. A. alone.

"Like hell," I answered, "come on." She refused, and pointed out that I was unarmed.

"So what?"

"Look at them," she whispered, pointing through the window at a sinister gang of Arabs assembled near the doorway. They held knives. "Leave it to me," she insisted, "I know how to handle them."

Valour followed ardour out of the barred window.

"Look straight ahead of you," she cautioned as she locked the door behind me.

Armed Arabs stood along the staircase, in the hallway, outside the door, and more were squatting in the street. With eyes fixed firmly ahead and swallowing my Adam's apple, I attempted a nonchalant saunter towards the bus station. I was perspiring freely in the cool of the early morning sunshine, at each step expecting a well-deserved knife in my dishonourable back. I sat on the back seat of the Tel Aviv bus for a whole hour, awaiting its departure, puzzling how that slip of a girl could so confidently handle the situation. Perhaps it had happened to her before. Or was it just that she knew the owners of the hotel and spoke Arabic. Back in T. A. I reassured myself with a hearty breakfast, and resolved I would never again make the mistake of wandering unarmed into that sort of nest.

Our week was up, our desert destiny remembered, and we turned away from artificiality. At Lydda we hitch-hiked a lift to the Nile Delta in a Lockheed Hudson which carried out a protracted antisubmarine patrol on the way, low over the sea a hundred miles offshore, being without a Mae West I was on tenterhooks. A week after our return 33 Squadron moved up through the desert to Misurata, not far from Tripoli, to support the Sicily invasion which started a fortnight later. We patrolled daily out into the ocean over the mighty convoys pummelling across to the European mainland, and the German Air Force stayed away.

Misurata was a handful of battered Italian villas and shops, but our encampment sat some distance outside the town alongside a small oasis, a clump of trees and crops laboriously watered by biblical methods. The "farmer", a charming young Senussi, used equipment consisting of a quantity of rope, a donkey, and a well with buckets. The donkey, haltered and blindfolded, stumbled round and round in well-beaten circles, raising bucketsful of water from the well; as the bucket reached ground level it was tripped, to spill its contents into a small reservoir from which it flowed along narrow channels to irrigate the land. The farmer thereupon lowered his bucket again and off the donkey went into its orbit. We watched hour after idle hour. Any excitement had passed us by and all we could do was wait for something to happen, maybe a summons to Italy where the Allies were now landing.

Until one morning as I slid from my camp-bed, a noise from under it caused me to bend down to investigate. A snake was coiled cosily beneath where my head had lain a few moments earlier. It had obviously come in for the warmth.

"Bloody snake!" I yelled as I rushed from the tent. My five tentmates were close on my tail.

"Shoot the bloody thing," counselled one.

"What if you miss, or only wound him and infuriate him?" warned a second.

"Bash him with a stick," a third advised.

While the conference continued I grabbed a spare tent-pole, seven or eight feet long, and prodded the reptile to encourage it to shove off; it hissed angrily. Cautiously I persevered, until obligingly it wrapped itself round the pole, yard after yard of the thing, it seemed. Gingerly I carried it out of the tent, fixed by its baleful eye. The Senussi came tearing across, grabbed the pole from me and raced back to his little oasis. Culling two large stones from the low wall around his property, he crushed the snake's head between them, while we looked on with hanging jaw. He looked up with a delighted smile to explain that the creature's bite was fatal to man or beast. It was fully six feet long, as thick as a man's wrist, and beautifully marked.

A great comfort to some of our lonelier airmen was an old girl of about seventy, an ancient shrivelled Arab woman clad in dirty rags, who used to come to the camp from the nearby township to take away our dirty laundry. Misurata Lil, as the aged crone became known, must have had some really interesting conversations in the tents where she lingered fifteen minutes or more. But in between sporadic peaks of despair at our sexual frustration, most of us had become almost conditioned to our enforced celibacy. As well, the brash individualism of a few months earlier had melted down to a kind of uniform insanity. No more did one see crazed Wing Commanders in pink hunting coats, nor pongo types (soldiers) roaming the desert in full-length sheepskin coats. With the departure of our Battle of Britain CO a regime had come to an end, and that which followed was more stifling; there was no consolation for the rigours of our desert life. One by one the great men continued to depart, and new, inexperienced pilots flooded in, so that by August 1943 only a handful of us remained out of those who had flown on the Squadron the previous year. The war was moving still further away and our sojourn became increasingly aimless. Sooner or later they would call us to battle . . . or were we to be left to rot as part of the desert garrison? My first year of exile had passed slowly, but I was now nearer home than at any time since arriving in Africa, and my thoughts turned constantly to the day I would return to England. Yet our airmen's songs were those of exile, concocted by men sentenced to the long four-year spells of foreign service which were the pre-1939 norm:

They say there's a troopship just leaving Bombay
Bound for old Blighty's shore,
Heavily laden with time-expired men
Bound for the land they adore.

There's many an airman just finishing his time,
Many a twerp signing on.
You'll get no promotion
This side of the ocean
So cheer up my lads, bless 'em all.

And so on, inconsequential jingle roared out in moments of shared misery. "Shaibah Blues" was sobbed with a chorus which implored the lecherous old homegoing boat to roll on. Another song indicated the fatal resignation of the airmen:

Fly high, fly low, wherever we go,
33 Squadron will never say No.

The author of one song, which lauded the licentious glories of a fabulous courtesan, name of Salome, was expert, at least theoretically, in an astonishing variety of lovemaking techniques which he attributed to her. The catalogue of her talents was such that for each day of the week she provided an entirely different and often original menu for satisfying her clientele. Possibly the author was a medical man, for he deployed a deep knowledge of the female anatomy, and spared little to the imagination in describing its most private workings. Another favourite song boasted the chorus:

Cats on the rooftops, cats on the tiles,
Cats with syphilis, cats with piles,
Cats with their   (rear quarters) wreathed in smiles
As they revel in the joys of fornication.

Obviously the libidinous felines were regarded as paragons of uninhibited sexuality. On the same note was a parody of a more famous song:

I don't want to join the Air Force,
I don't want to go to war;
I'd rather hang around
Piccaddilly Underground,
Living on the earnings of a high-born lady . . .

And there was . . .

. . . a street in Cairo
Full of syph and shame,
Sharia El-Berka
Is its f-ing name;
Russian, French and Greek bints (girls)
All around I see,
Come all ye Air Force men,
Abide with me!

Singing the depraved verses with gusto seemed to achieve an odd inverted satisfaction, as though jeering at the sexual act. Although they were delivered lightheartedly, combined with our extremely obscene language, anti-clerical attitudes and profane jokes, they represented extroversions from the emotional tensions of exile accentuated by physical and spiritual hardship, underpinned by daily danger. The knowledge that we were all in it together diluted the impact of the awfulness. Sharing adversity welded us together into a camaraderie which helped sustain us — however dispirited a group may become, there seems invariably to be one who can muster the courage and optimism to cheer the others. Such a one was Tubby Lewis, a jovial Welshman, who would challenge you to and beat you at any card game, or draughts, or chess, shove ha'penny or matchbox rugby, or any other of the innocent schoolboyish games we invented to help wile away the long hours of boredom and the more miserable aspects of our exile.

"Poverty!" he would exclaim loudly if he made a mistake at draughts. And "Joobs!" Nobody ever found out what "Joobs" were, possibly something Celtic. Tubby's self-denigratory expressions grew with his increasing insanity, and the mighty imprecation of "Pov-Joobs!" rocketing round the canvas walls of the Mess tent was soon followed by an impassioned "Death! where is thy sting!" Like the rest of us, he was "shwyea magnoon" — desert-happy, the Service circumlocution for a bit potty.

At about this time the authorities, conscious perhaps that their men's breasts were innocent still of the humblest patch of colour, issued a medal to all and sundry. Every man-jack who wore uniform, or was to wear it, at any time or place during the War, however unwarlike his station might be, became the proud owner of a red, dark blue and light blue ribbon, the 1939-45 Star. Inevitably, its commonplaceness rapidly gave rise to yet another mocking song, sung to the tune of "Alice Blue Gown":

120

In my '39–45 Star,
It's the best bloomin' medal by far,
I've got one on my chest
And I've one on my vest
And one on my pyjamas when I go to rest . . .

. . . and so on, ending up with

But I'd rather not share it
With the millions who wear it —
My '39–45 Star.

Our own heroic part in the invasion of Italy, which consisted of flying protective patrols over the convoys from North Africa to Sicily, earned us another medal, the Italy Star, which we thought was a great joke.

Tripoli, hardly marked by the battles which had rolled over it, boasted white civilians, Italian settler relics who were strangely unwelcoming, considering we had liberated them. I thought they must be sick of the sight of military uniforms and just wanted to get on with their ice-cream and a bit of opera. Hopefully anticipating a modicum of fraternisation, I had taken the trouble to learn some Italian out of a Teach-Yourself book, but it was never put to the test.

Only four of us pilots remained from earlier days, and the time came when we were posted "Tour expired." After a "tour" of operations, usually two hundred hours of operational sorties for the fighter-pilot, he was given a few months on a non-operational flying job, which

121

enabled him to keep his hand in but his life intact, ahead of his second "tour." Here, belatedly, was to be my chance to acquire the true flying skill which had so far eluded me.

CHAPTER
SIX

Soft Living

At El Firdan, an elegant airfield alongside the Suez Canal, just to the north of Ismailia, I joined No. 26 Anti-Aircraft Cooperation Unit. The pilots were nearly all tour-expired operational types rather than the cluster of failures, who we called dead-beats, I had expected, and there was consequently a squadron-like atmosphere which was good for the morale. Even more unexpected was the absence of any discipline as I had known it, and the free and easy cosiness was remarkable after the toughness of squadron and desert existence. Could Air Force men really have been living like this the whole time we were suffocating and half-starving in the sand? There was food and a Viennese Jewish cook to dish it up, most appetisingly. Three-course meals twice daily, as well as a mammoth breakfast, and second helpings whenever you wanted. I soon began regaining the nine kilos lost in the desert. The Mess was built of concrete, and as comfortable as you like, but the rest of the camp was tented. I had never seen such tents; they were titivated beyond belief. It was done like this:

At a snap of the fingers a gang of otherwise unemployed Egyptian labourers arrived armed with spades. Sand flew in all directions until there was a hole in the sand into which a one-hundred-and-eighty-pound tent could fit. Unshaven and dressed in dirty gelabeias they worked at terrifying speed.

"Salaam l'Allah, waladi ya waladi," they sang as they bagged the sand into canvas sacks with which they then lined the walls of the pit they had dug. Next, they paved the floor with concrete slabs, then up went the tent, its walls resting at ground level, so that you stepped down into a luxurious abode that was no less than ten feet high from floor to ridge, and amazingly cool.

"Salaam l'Allah, waladi," they chortled, sweeping the spare sand from the floor before heaving in our bedding and kitbags. Coloured cotton from the bazaar at Ismailia disguised the sandbag walls, and by then electric cabling had been pushed through the sand to provide switched-on lighting after a year of hurricane lamps. "Furniture" was contrived out of wooden and cardboard boxes, and all our spare gear stowed tidily away behind a fly-sheet extension at the tent's rear. Six of us shared a tent of the same size in the desert; here we were only two, in surroundings that were spacious, clean, and in every way a debonair accessory to the new comfortable life. Cheap rugs thrown down on the concrete slabs completed the air of luxury, of which I began to feel slightly ashamed.

I had hardly settled in when I was asked, "Now what about a spot of leave, old man?" Conscience-smitten, I entrained again for Cairo, and thence Tel Aviv, where

I started replacing my paperback library, stolen somewhere between Misurata and the Delta. Impassioned by my still emaciated frame the girl in the bookshop lured me to a quiet park where as soon as dusk fell she set about seducing me. My response was sadly inadequate, due perhaps to the long period of enforced abstention, her inappropriate body odour, or the considerable indication of moustache atop her upper lip.

Two days later I rediscovered the little village mentally noted on my earlier visit, prowled around its few dusty lanes, and was enchanted. I ate lunch in a circular concrete restaurant. Upstairs they rented out a few unadorned concrete cells with roughly-whitewashed ceiling and walls. I took one, and went back to collect my things. The denizens of the village were mostly continental Jews, accustomed to a cafe existence, and I found that I had located myself at the hub, as well as the perimeter, of their social life. The public gaiety and relaxation represented something quite unfamiliar to me. They played cards and dominoes, or merely gossiped over interminable cups of coffee. There was an Air Force radio station on the outskirts of the village, so they were accustomed to our uniform, and I aroused neither curiosity nor interest. A few Arabs frequented the restaurant, not at all like the Egyptians, but handsome men wearing pure white headdresses surmounted by a cord band; instead of the Egyptian gelabeia they wore the baggy trousers into which their Prophet Mohammed would one day be reborn of man, and European-style jackets. Some were

125

sons of the men who had fought with Lawrence a generation earlier, one war back.

On somebody's radio Churchill's rolling rhythms majestically informed the world of Italy's capitulation, and there it was in the newspapers, "Italien hatt surrendierte." My week passed quickly and I was glad to get back to the airplanes, for here was my opportunity to teach myself to fly, to do it so well that I'd love it. For Allen James had got things the wrong way round. You cannot love a hobby or a job which you don't do well, but if you do it well you may begin to love it. His well-meaning had however stuck in my mind, and now I had my chance.

There was plenty of flying, in clapped-out old Hurricanes, bumping in hot turbulence up and down a predetermined line, while gunners aimed at your reciprocal course; or haring up and down between two points, twenty-five thousand feet up, while they ranged on you. At the end of each trip there was enough fuel for fifteen minutes of aerobatics, and in my months at El Firdan I taught myself a good deal of what there was to know about flying Hurricanes, rolling and looping calmly and with a precision I never had in those earlier days when the control-column was frantically stirred round the cockpit. Try as I would, I still could not manage a decent vertical climbing roll, but not many pilots could. I developed a pièce-de-résistance which did my morale no end of good, a dive taking me to a few feet above the ground at three hundred and twenty miles an hour, at which speed I raced across the airfield, then up into a looping arc at the top of which, at perhaps eighteen hundred feet, I pushed the stick across so that the plane half-rolled to straight and level flight, before pushing the wing over and nose down with the throttle closed, to screw in to the tight "split-arse" approach of a landing fighter. Of course it was blatant showing-off, but it was expected of us and the ground crew loved it. Thus did I first start cutting an aviatorial figure as I perfected that manoeuvre and one or two others besides. I became and knew I was a good pilot, a confident pilot, and began to love flying, so that I was never happier than when airborne, and hated days when there wasn't a trip. I was a professional.

From somewhere or other our Flight-Commander, a burly New Zealander, acquired a Hart, the Hurricane's biplane precursor, a lovely and easy plane to handle, except that its brakes were located somewhere at the top of and beyond the rudder pedals. He eventually wrote the Hart off when landing in a stiff crosswind, which necessitates full rudder application to prevent the plane following its natural tendency to yaw into wind; unfortunately his foot got stuck in the rudder apparatus so that he applied not only full rudder but full brake as well, so that the Hart slewed wildly round in ever diminishing circles until, as we used to say, it disappeared up its own orifice, with him in the middle of a noisy jumble of wreckage, confusion and sand. It was difficult for him to say much to me when next day, after a particularly spectacular beat-up, I sliced the wing tip off my Hurricane while taxiing in. My over-elation had gone to my head and made me clumsy.

The ex-desert pilots were still sand-happy. They included diminutive Napier, who in his spare moments walked round with peaked cap pulled down over his enormous luminous eyes murmuring, "Momma, momma, come and feel this cat's ass. It's so god-damned smoo-oo-ooth!" And Cairns, a large, bluff, simple soul who, having also suffered in the desert, had conjured up a wonderful idea for pleasing the troops and at the same time making his fortune. He would can a certain part of the female anatomy and market it in outlandish regions. He had already devised a suitable advertising slogan: "Cairn's Canned C----; A Poke In Every Pot!"

The Flight-Commander crashed again and this time made a thorough job of it, writing himself off as well as his plane; the first death for some time. The charm had deserted him. "The higher the fewer," intoned Napier. "The greater the lesser. The faster the later." There was a kind of insane logic in it.

I was promoted to Chiefy, the title reserved for Flight-Sergeants, though mostly applied to that cheerful and highly-skilled band of men who formed the backbone of the RAF — the old-sweat engine fitters and riggers, armourers and electricians and maintenance kings who devoted their lives to the Service. In those days many of them seemed to be of a type — from poor homes (why else join up in peacetime?), stunted in stature, tough through survival, wizened and wrinkled by tropical service, skilled beyond belief, philosophical through experience, humorous because of familiarity with adversity. The "regulars" served perhaps twenty or twenty-five years before attaining the rank now thrust on me after three years. "Bloody 'Chiefy' Naydler," said one of them in a friendly enough way, "Why, mate, you haven't been in long enough to know whether your (rear end) is punched, bored, drilled or countersunk!" I could not disagree. But worse was to follow because before long a further automatic promotion elevated me to the dizzy height of Warrant Officer, something most of the Chiefies could never attain. I could now rise no further unless into the ranks of commissioned officers, but my career to then had included recurring encounters with authority which had led to my being considered a rebel, unfit to assume fuller responsibilities, though perhaps another minor discouragement was that my father happened to be an enemy alien. Never, with the more ambitious airmen, could I truthfully say, "They wanted me to go for an officer but I said no I'd rather stay with the lads."

Transit camps excepted, because they were invariably demoralising slums, the first-class self-discipline on every RAF unit I knew stemmed from work. Whether servicing or flying airplanes, the job was done seriously and with total dedication and responsibility. But on the ground, when off duty, the wartime Air Force insisted on relaxing and conducting itself in accordance with its own integrity, anything superficial to the working discipline being considered "bullshit", superfluous, no matter from what elevated source it might emanate. The morality tended to include anything faintly smacking of the clerical as superfluous.

After some time at El Firdan, during which I swept low over the Gizeh pyramids and sphinx on more hot, bumpy calibration runs than I care to remember, a small contingent of us flew to the Lebanon to undertake the same task there in cooperation with the Army, which was training for an imaginative sweep through Turkey into the Balkans. It was good to escape desert flying conditions, where an hour at five hundred or a thousand feet was exhausting, especially to the reddened raw eyes. Yatte, a broad field between the Lebanon and Anti-Lebanon mountain ranges, was not more than a mile from Baalbeck, where stood the ruins of the Roman temple of Heliopolis, City of the Sun, five thousand feet above sea level but another five thousand below the crests of the parallel mountain ranges separated by the wide Bekaa Valley; at its northern end was the Turkish frontier. Baalbeck, a delightful village, had recently been taken over by the Army to whose care we were entrusted. They ferried us between the village and the field in lorries, from which we looked down at the locals, who looked up curiously at us with our strange flying paraphernalia. There were fair-skinned, ruddy-complexioned, English-looking girls with names like Leonora, relics of the Crusaders. We were neither crusading nor did we stay long enough to have a chance of repeating so delightful a bit of history, for within a few days it started snowing, then it froze, snowed some more and froze some more, so that to prepare the Hurricanes for flying became increasingly difficult. Some of the ground crew had had experience of similar conditions in Russia with the Hurricanes

130

which had operated from there a year or so earlier. They improvised tents round the planes' noses, and beneath them lit fires to unfreeze the engines. It was decided to fly the planes to Beirut, on the warm coastal strip, and to operate from there. It was only a matter of twenty minutes to fly over the mountains. We must not be grounded, as we were also serving as an operational unit in case of German counter-attack through Turkey down into the Levant. There remained the problem of getting the planes to Beirut when the whole of the Bekaa Valley lay under several inches of frozen snow.

I decided on a take-off along the skating-rink of a runway, theorising that with sufficient taxiing speed the flow of air over the rudder would enable me to maintain control as I made for the take-off spot, as long as I avoided using the brakes, as that would inevitably cause a skid. My Hurricane was prepared for flight and started up; it took over fifteen minutes to warm the engine to a safe temperature. At fifty miles an hour I gunned the plane along the ice with its tail in the air. The rudder responded to the controls and in a gentle arc I brought her round until I was pointing along the runway, then without pausing I opened the throttle fully, the Hurricane responded like a bird, and we were airborne off the skating-rink without a trace of a skid. I flew straight towards Beirut, flat out until I could throttle back at eleven thousand feet, clear of the snowy mountains which seemed as if they wanted to reach out and grab me, then a slow dive down their western flanks brought me over Beirut ten minutes later. The airport had very short runways, with the town on three

131

sides of it and the beach on the fourth, so one had to approach with wheels and flaps down, like a Fleet Air Arm plane approaching a carrier. The danger of such an approach is dual — you are utterly vulnerable and may get shot down on your run-in; and if your engine fails you haven't a hope. Both those reasons explain the fighter-pilot's conventional split-arse corkscrewing approach.

The other Hurricanes were close behind, and for three happy weeks we flew from Beirut and revelled in the amenities of its sophisticated luxuries. During the period I flew a Hurricane back to El Firdan for repairs, returning with a replacement which had to be delivered to Haifa, in Palestine. I was just airborne, my undercarriage still down, when a spray of glycol smothered the cockpit and me. That highly flammable liquid was used to cool the engine, and its escape meant that the temperature gauge whizzed rapidly off the clock. I whipped up the undercarriage, to crash-land in the sand surrounding the airfield, to put the plane down if the engine caught fire. At ten feet above the ground I flew in a tight right-handed circle, hoping to reach the end of one of the runways. The cockpit was filled with fumes even though the canopy was still open, the doomed engine sprayed the windscreen with oil so that I could not see ahead. I craned over the side of the cockpit and my goggles were spattered. I used the back of my gloves to wipe them clear as I craned for one of the runway ends. The minute or so before I lined one of them up seemed an eternity, then I slammed down the undercarriage and switched off, touching down across a stiff wind without flaps, which act as an air brake and also reduce stalling speed. The Hurricane careered along the runway at a rate of knots, screeching widly as the brakes bit.

I knew there was a large "frying-pan" at the end of the runway, and reckoned that by the time we reached it my speed would be down to forty miles an hour, when I would ground-loop the plane — by applying full rudder and brake on one side simultaneously the plane would swing violently round through one hundred and eighty degrees and stop dead. It was a manoeuvre to be used in emergency only, but a trained pilot was more expensive (if not more valuable) than the undercarriage of the plane which a ground-loop was likely to remove. Unhappily the frying-pan was occupied by a parked Maryland bomber. There was no choice. The Hurricane tore off the end of the runway into the sand. I let it carry on until just before the sandbagged wall which served as protection for the buildings behind it from the slipstream of aircraft taking off, then ground-looped. Flames were licking back from the now molten engine, but the bloodwagon (ambulance) and fire engine were already alongside, and the latter was busy spraying everything with foam, including me as I climbed smartly from the cockpit and placed a distance between the plane and me. The engine was hissing balefully but the fire did not spread to the wings, where the petrol tanks were located. The bloodwagon conducted me back to the Flight Tent rather like a conquering hero. The Hurricane proved to be one hundred per cent except for a new engine and a new glycol-tank filler-cap, pierced by the airman who had filled it — as was the normal custom he had used his screwdriver blade to administer the final tightening of the cap, instead of the tommy-bar provided for the purpose. This had been done so many times before but this last occasion had seen the blade pierce the cap, allowing the glycol to escape and the engine to boil over and catch fire. I had been carrying mail for the Haifa contingent in the gun compartment of the port side wing. It was rescued and transferred into the wing of another Hurricane in which I took off and flew to Ramat David, the Haifa airfield, arriving just before nightfall. Next morning I left for Beirut, and no sooner was I airborne . . .

This time, the wing panel where the mail had been extracted had not been properly screwed home by the rigger, flying off with a plop just as the plane left the ground, to lurch unhappily in a couple of feet of airspace. The runway was long, and it was easy to make an instant decision to cut the throttle and abort the take-off. By the end of the runway my speed was less than sixty miles an hour and I could ease the Hurricane round the tarmac perimeter track until it came to a safe stop, slewing into the soft mud at the verge. That made twice in two days. I should have known what was coming next.

Over Beirut the next day, after a trip to the Bekaa Valley, I studied the landing-T, which indicates the direction in which to land, along the upright and towards the bar; it is laid on the ground outside the control-tower, made up of white wooden sections. The windsock hung limply, but such slight wind as there was indicated that the landing-T was pointing down wind; normally, unless for some very unusual reason, take-off and landing are always into wind. Landing down wind on any runway is not recommended, but on Beirut's tiny runway, with the town immediately on the outskirts of the airfield, it was going to be a delicate operation indeed. I orbited to discover why I had to land down wind, and saw a gang of labourers working in close vicinity to the end of the runway where I would touch down if landing in the right direction. With no radio whereby to call up the tower I took the precaution of making a third orbit, half expecting the duty pilot, which is what we called the flight controller, to change the landing-T, but he didn't. Okay, a down wind landing.

The Hurricane drifted, and drifted, and drifted until it touched down about halfway along the runway. Because of the buildings at its far end there was no room to follow the overshoot procedure, that is open up and go round again, so I had to brake hard, harder, hardest. I ran out of runway and into the sand, just past the men-at-work. Never mind, I was only doing thirty, I'd ground-loop the bitch as I did at El Firdan, when something happened, I didn't know what, except that there was an impact of sorts, the Hurricane's rear end lifted infinitely gently, her nose pushed into the sand, I was hanging forward, then the sky disappeared.

When I recovered my senses I realised I was upside down, hanging in darkness in my safety-harness, with sand all round me. The engine was silent. I switched off ignition. Amid a jabber of Arabic the plane began to wobble. The labourers had hold of one wing and were trying to cartwheel the plane upright, but they hadn't a hope of budging its seven tons, and only succeeded in swinging me around, bashing me against the cockpit sides, the control column and the dashboard. I released the buckle of my harness, to plop onto my head in the sand and bash myself some more. My face, up to the mouth in sand, was bearing the weight of my body. Trapped in an area measuring three feet by two feet by three feet there was no space to move my limbs. I was in my tiny upside-down prison less than half-an-hour, before the side of the cockpit was hatcheted away and I was dragged out, spitting sand as I bounced to my feet, full of bonhomie and assuring the ambulance-men that I was absolutely fine. My trousers were torn at the knee where a bit of blood showed. Notwithstanding my protests they bundled me off to the hospital from where, after a thorough overhaul and the application of plasters to some superficial cuts, I was sent home and told to go to bed early. My charm had survived.

I awoke a few hours later in a muck sweat, trembling violently with delayed shock. Riotously my imagination addressed itself to my predicament had the Hurricane caught fire — like the one two days earlier. I was up at first light, long before the world was awake, running down to the Flight where the Hurricanes stood. I was airborne up the mountainside and over into the Valley and back before breakfast — an instinctive reaction, without which I had little doubt that my flying career would have ended there and then, my flying nerve destroyed for ever.

An apology from a shamefaced duty pilot explained that at the moment of my arrival the previous afternoon he had been unable to attend to his landing-T because he was on the telephone taking down a gale warning. The gale had arrived as I was landing, the cause of the Hurricane drifting so far. The Court of Inquiry, held to determine the cause of the loss of one Hurricane aircraft, established that a leg of the plane had hit the protruding inches of a submerged forty-gallon oildrum with considerable impact, throwing the plane into a forward somersault. The duty pilot was court-martialled and sent away in disgrace. Had I failed to carry out the full drill prior to landing, which included lowering one's seat, I would have taken the Hurricane's seven tons on my spinal column and no amount of charm would have saved my life. Instead, the weight had been taken by the protective armoured plate. A large lorry bore away the wreckage, while I murmured sadly at my folly.

Beirut was fascinating, our weeks there a rest-cure. Like an exotic, miniature Brussels set on the edge of the Mediterranean, even in winter it seemed to be bathed in permanent sunshine. You could swim in the sea, gallop along the broad beach, ski in the nearby mountains, or just loaf around the town enjoying the shops, cafés, bars and cabarets. The French influence lent a chic urbanity which knocked off a few of our raw edges, and swiftly we became adept at nonchalant lounging in the mornings in elegant little cafés where the confectionery was suffocatingly delectable and the café-crème superb; and at night in soigné cabarets where exciting belly-dancers, superbly cosmeticised, allowed you to buy them champagne after their song-and-dance routine.

A local family with three unmarried daughters adopted me, and we spent several unhappy hours in their drawing-room, sipping arak, the local aniseed drink, in glum silence. Quite simply, none of us had anything to say. It might have been different had Mummy and Daddy left us alone for an hour or so. Even half-an-hour. But not for a minute did they. I expect those three girls are still sitting in stony, unmarried silence. It wasn't as if Daddy didn't know, for at the end of each particularly prolonged silence came his faithful observation: "Another split one is born", meaning that silence betokens the birth of yet another female child, not a sought-after event out there. But a private home made an acceptable change from bars, and lent a small sense of belonging. I was beginning to mellow and even pondered whether any of the Headquarters warriors had, like me, earned their cream buns.

The Beirut idyll ended with a transfer to the Ramat David detachment on the outskirts of Haifa. Thence in our free time, of which there was plenty, we pop-popped down Mount Carmel on the bus to town, where young Jews and Jewesses actually danced the hora in the streets. Here, as completely if less intensely, our uniforms constituted a strong taboo on any kind of relationship with the civilian population.

A bus ride took us to Nazareth, which even in those unlikely days was full of tourists. The pretty, steep, dusty village of ancient sandstone and pompous acolyte-officials burnt under a clear sky of that deep blue which only the Mediterranean lands produce. Somehow or other we found ourselves in a large marquee where young Polish girls were holding a strange exhibition of their national costume and custom. They were tender and sweet and younger than us; one took me confidingly by the hand to show me her family photograph album. Her hair was long and fair, and she wore the Polish national costume of black velvet skirt, white frilled blouse, and short green and red tunic trimmed with lace. At twenty-three I had outgrown the incredible idyllic romanticism of youth but was not ready to be the father-figure which, exiled at the age of seventeen, she seemed to be looking for. Yet it was a gentle and touching occasion. Heaven knows how we managed to converse, but at all events I understood that she was not permitted to leave the camp in which she lived on an island on Lake Tiberias, not even to meet a father-figure, which role I was by then very nearly prepared to assume for the sweet, innocent child.

Sayed Harif, a cultured European-clad Arab, a Coptic Christian, took us to his home where his mother entertained us to tea. White and square from without, decorated with delicate wrought-iron window-bars and doorway, within it was cool and shady, with dark walls and marble floors. We sat on the edge of elaborate green-cushioned chairs, while his mother, a slight, elegant, upright figure in black robes and a lace shawl, presided over the dignified ceremony, pouring tea through a complicated system of strainers. We drank it milkless through a lemon slice, accompanied by small sweet biscuits, and carried on a difficult conversation through Sayed's interpretation, as his mother spoke only Arabic. The occasion had the quality of a serene, other-worldly vignette, and made me conscious of my immature clumsiness.

One of the pilots, who had been at Ramat David too long, tired of the endless celibacy and married a local girl in Jerusalem, where we attended the nuptials. At a dance that evening we enjoyed dancing with the civilian ladies who were our fellow-guests, but at precisely midnight the band played "Goodnight Sweetheart", decently followed by the national anthem, then withdrew. The party looked like breaking up until someone desperately thrust open the lid of the piano and steered me to it. For some years my effective repertoire had been "I'll See You Again" and "Torno a Sorrento", both in the key of C which has no confusing black notes, and which I now played one after the other, the other after the one, through into the small hours while the RAF celebrants waltzed determinedly on, enlocked with their unaccustomed females. After an endless session of three-four time I was politely asked whether I couldn't play something else. I couldn't, but inspired by the oblique compliment and reluctant to admit my limitations, I embarked upon heavy rhythmic thumps at the lower notes, aiming in the approximate direction of foxtrot tempo. Even to me the noise seemed appalling, especially when my right hand, carried away, started tinkling out of control up and down the top half of the bewildered keyboard. Generous supplies of refreshment encouraged me to hammer execrably on, perspiring freely as my gusto increased, until I observed with concern that the ivory veneers of the keys were actualy flying off in several directions, starting with middle C round which my tunes largely revolved. As the bits accumulated they were neatly stacked by my mates, but inevitably the situation came to the notice of the management and the piano lid was closed with such firmness that I narrowly avoided grievous damage to the fingertips. Though exhausted for several days I had at least enjoyed an important if brief moment of artistic success.

Returning to El Firdan in a powerful limousine driven by a mad Brigadier at breakneck speed across the tacky, black, winding ribbon that served as a road through the Sinai Desert, tall waves of sand piled high on either side were punctuated by rocky ravines of pale brown sandstone, burning hot, uninhabited and uninhabitable, and infinitely more formidable than they appeared from the air.

Our Army Cooperation was now directed towards Suez, at the south entrance to the Canal, over which I flew interminably. It was all right until you had to do a low-level run, when the heat was such that it was imperative to fly with the cockpit canopy open in order to get air, whereupon the stench from the town flooded upwards in such unbearable waves that you had to slide the canopy forward to keep out the smell, when the heat became so intolerable . . . But on the way home there was ample time for aerobatics, and although it extended the journey a little I looped and rolled the sixty-odd miles in a state of confident bliss. In a communal life, the state of a fighter-pilot when airborne alone satisfies the innate need for privacy. He is unchallenged king of a vast spatial empire whose three dimensions he rules self-confidently and with no responsibility other than to himself.

By now, almost two years had passed since leaving England, and whilst my thoughts were less regularly directed at the day of my return, their intensity was greater than in the first year of exile, when there was so much novelty to engage a young man's attention. Rumours abounded of repatriation after two years overseas. The flattery of the posting I received therefore eluded me when in late May 1944 I was perfunctorily handed a chit inscribed: "Report to AHQ Delhi, India, for posting to RAF Burma as experienced operational pilot."

CHAPTER
SEVEN

"Desertion"

The name Burma filled me with deep and genuine horror. Wartime propaganda had driven home the awfulness of conditions out there, not least the unrelenting savagery of the Japanese, quite apart from such minor considerations as snakes, jungle, and dread tropical diseases. It was about the last place I wanted to go; another four thousand miles further from home. I did not mind a second operational tour, indeed I welcomed it now that I really knew how to fly, but why not in Europe where there was still plenty of action in Italy, with a second front in France not far away. I shuddered at the cruel blow, scarcely alleviated by the detailed instructions which followed, to report to Almaza . . . Almaza of all the places I had never expected to see again; that was really rubbing salt in the wound. Alcatraz, then Burma, came as near as made no difference to a slow, painful death sentence. It was what we airmen called "the dreaded end!" Reeling back I groaned inwardly and hated the guts of the cosy headquarters cream bun-eating bastards who had cooked this one up. I had a companion in adversity. Wuffles Mowbray had done a tour on a desert squadron, been posted to 26 AACU, attained the mighty rank of Warrant Officer, and was now in the same boat with me. Mowbray could both talk and drink the hind legs off a donkey. "Rot their horrid cotton socks!" he maledicted on receiving the news. Sick at heart we packed and jorneyed to the dreaded transit camp.

Except that the fat Commandant had been buried, the place hadn't changed a bit. But we had, and it didn't take long to discover the date of our departure for Burma and apply for leave to fill in the interval. In Alexandria for five vehement days we gave vent to our unhappiness in a glorious non-stop drinking session, initiated by bottles of breakfast in the frisky bug-ridden rooms of a sleazy hotel, rising at the crack of noon, then starting the day really right with a hefty pre-lunch orgy. Whenever possible we altercated with authority in the shape of the Military Police, heedless of the consequences. In the RAF language of the time, we pressed on regardless, and truly couldn't have cared less. On reflection, though I doubt whether without Mowbray's influence I would have behaved thus, in the circumstances we did the only sensible thing there was to do.

June 5th 1944 saw us aboard an Imperial Airways flying-boat alongside Gezireh, on the Nile, where stood the Sporting Club beloved of the chairborne warriors. During twenty-four hours' recuperative sleep which followed I was vaguely conscious of refuelling halts in the Dead Sea, on the lake at Habbaniyah in Iraq, and at Basra at the head of the Persian Gulf. I came to when we were pitched ashore for the night into a sumptuous air-conditioned hotel at Bahrain Island, the hottest place ever: it was midsummer. The air-conditioning induced a kind of cool fungoid moistness reflected in the exclusive bottle of Turkish beer which cost five shillings, which was exactly fifteen times the normal price. The next day saw the lap accomplished across the Horn of Arabia, along the muddy Iranian and Baluchistani littoral fronting a dead flat, glittering Arabian Sea, and thus towards Karachi.

Shortly before noon the Captain invited us into his deafening cabin and motioned me into the co-pilot's seat, allowing me to take the controls while he twiddled with the radio. Suddenly his face assumed an astonished expression, and putting on the spare headphones I listened with him to the BBC. "During last night 1,500 aircraft of Bomber Command dropped more than 5,000 tons of bombs on coastal batteries in Northern France. During the night more than 1,000 troop carriers and gliders of the United States 9th Army Air Force and the RAF flew paratroops and airborne infantry into the zone of operations. Mass airborne landings have already been made behind the enemy lines. The mightiest armada of all time, comprising more than 4,000 ships with several thousand smaller craft, sustained by 11,000 aircraft, is landing the invading Allied army on beaches in Normandy. Shortly after dawn more than 1,000 American heavy bombers and waves of medium bombers took up the attack. Landings on the beaches are proceeding at various points on a broad front."

145

We grinned at each other, wondrously happy, shook hands, then I went back excitedly to tell the other passengers the news. It had come at last, the second front we had so long awaited, and surely it could not now be long before under overwhelming pressure from West and East at the same time, Germany and her satellites were brought to their knees and the interminable war came to an end. It did not cross my mind that some cream buneaters might have been at work. A little later the Captain told me of the German V-1 "doodlebugs", news of which had never reached us in the Middle East, and which I found difficult to imagine.

At Karachi we were hauled off the flying-boat by an efficient wingless Squadron Leader who, heedless of our protests and posting chit, ordered us to a transit camp. Those bloody transit camps were everywhere. "But we're posted to Burma as experienced —"

"Experienced nothing! You all arrive with the same chits. AHQ India comes later. Don't you realise that jungle warfare is quite different from the desert? We'll be sending you to a Jungle Training Course as soon as we can." Our chits were confiscated and once again we were transit camp prisoners. Admittedly, Melir was umpteen times less intolerable than Alcatraz, although at that time of the year it was swept day and night by a hot dusty wind straight off the Sind Desert, which after a week became a trial to the nerves. We sought solace and succour in Karachi, a stifling and rather dirty town in those days, but where of all things I rediscovered Vimto, a favourite Lancashire boyhood beverage. By what stroke of genius or quirk of eccentricity had Vimto penetrated to that improbable spot! Our thirst was also alleviated by the char-wallahs who sold tea out of urns, in much the same way as the Cairenes at Almaza, but somehow less unwholesome. In the town we sauntered inquisitively, curious at the sacred white cows which wandered at will in and out of restaurants and shops, and intrigued at the communal laundry-pools where clothes were hammered clean against stone walls, a technique which certainly got the clothes pure, though their life must have been greatly curtailed. One rarely saw an Indian in other than spotless garb, perhaps a benefit of built-in obsolescence.

The other pilots in the camp were youngsters straight from Blighty and we didn't much appreciate being sent on a refresher course with them. So when after a month we were put on a train to the jungle camp somewhere near Bombay, we noticed with interest that by evening it had reached Lahore, considerably nearer to Delhi, where AHQ India was located, than to Bombay, on the first leg of a cumbersome journey which circumvented the enormous Sind Desert. After Mowbray and I had spent a day or two in Lahore resting, a kindly Lockheed Hudson pilot gave us a lift to Delhi, where we reported smartly to AHQ India, in accordance with our confiscated chit. It took a while to gain an audience with a be-winged Group Captain, whose main concern was to know how we had evaded the Karachi net. He took our explanation calmly enough, but regretted that we'd simply have to go to the Jungle Training School. Politely we reminded him that we'd been posted for service in Burma as experienced operational fighter pilots, that there was by all accounts a very nice war in Burma, and an obvious shortage of good pilots. There we were at Delhi, our acknowledged experience clearly obviating the need for any kind of course, unlike the other young men in the Karachi camp. Fifteen minutes of that maudlin stuff moved him but left him unconvinced. Ten minutes later we were constrained to play our trump card. If he felt obliged to refuse us an immediate posting to Burma he would be depriving some squadron of a couple of useful blokes but more, the RAF would have a couple of deserters on its hands for which he alone would be responsible, and what good would that do! We wanted to get to an operational squadron as soon as possible, do our second tour, then perhaps there'd be a chance of being repatriated. We were too old to be pitched in and out of transit camps and refresher courses. Tears could be seen welling into his steely eyes. It was true that Mowbray and I had seriously talked together about deserting rather than be mucked about any more, and of making our own way to Burma where perhaps we could talk sensibly to some responsive Squadron commander. The Group Captain turned to a tall, dark and handsome man who had been sitting quietly in a corner throughout the interview, smoking endless cigarettes. He wore the rings of a Squadron Leader. "What d'you make of them, Molly?" he asked, rather helplessly.

They went into a huddle.

"Okay, Molly," he said, "be it on your own head."

Molly Malone turned to us.

"I have a squadron down in the Arakan," he informed us. "That's the coast where India and Burma meet. It's not an RAF squadron — it's Indian Air Force. Most of the pilots and all of the men are Indians. We're operating in that region so you'll get your action. And if you'd like to come to us for a while I'd be glad to have you. Later, we can organise you a posting to a RAF squadron in Central Burma."

We took little time to accept the generous offer, while the Group Captain sighed and buzzed for his adjutant to prepare the necessary posting and travel chits. Animated, we trotted over to Molly Malone who wrote on part of his cigarette packet the magic words, "Singarbil, Agartala", tore the bit off and handed it to us. I was overcome with the unpronounceability of the words.

"We're at Singarbil in Nepal," he explained, "but you'll only be able to get as far as Agartala, where there's an airstrip used by Transport Command. When you get there, send us a signal and we'll send a gharry to pick you up. I shan't be there myself for another week so take your time. You have to go via Calcutta anyway — it's worth a visit."

What a king of a man, we thought.

Reaching Singarbil took more than a week, what with exploring a foetid pre-monsoon Delhi from which the cognoscenti had already withdrawn to the cool of the hills, hitch-hiking an air lift to Calcutta, and making cursory contact with that teeming microcosm. "Gradystone, Sahib", repeated the gharry-wallah who conducted us in his worn black vehicle to the Great Eastern Hotel, a Victorian monster reminiscent of St. Pancras Station, where we shared a room with two "pongos", another rude RAF word for Army officers, who didn't really smell. Chowringhee, Calcutta's Piccadilly, was fabulous. The density of population was unbelievable, but then the Indians tended to live — and die — on the streets, every one of which was drenched with a torrent of skinny, white-garbed men whose dark faces framed lurid mouths, stained red with the betel-nut they chewed and which they spat on to the pavements, dyeing them a rich crimson. It was evening, and mattresses were already appearing on the sidewalks, the home of countless thousands; it was said that in the early morning the night carts which removed the day's accumulation of dung also took away the corpses of those who had died in the night. Certainly I was to see emaciated bodies lying in the gutters looking dead, though apparently that was sometimes a beggar's trick.

The backsheesh of the Middle East was now buckshee. I had never been called "Effendi" in the former but for sure I was Sahib in the latter. The word means friend. Here was a huge metropolis where, if your skin was black, you could live in total anonymity, one of millions of unknown who looked the same, struggling to survive through sheer will-power, familiar with the starvation which resulted from incredible poverty, but still with the loin-fire of procreation stirring within you until your very death-gasp. India, tumultuous country of the Kama Sutra; of Vashti the fruitful, four-handed Vishnu, Rama-Deva, beautiful god

150

of loving, Shiva the destroyer, amorous Krishna, Brahma the ever-recurring; India, prolific begetter of vast human waste; India, teeming womb of the East; over-rich in human fertility, saturated with population, bloated with enfeebled essence, encrusted with genital gems, profligate in copulation, effusive in emotion, eternally enduring.

Thus down Chowringhee's broad childbearing thighs we made our gaping way, past American soldiers squatting on the sidewalks, calling out hopefully to impossible peasant women with babes astride their ragclad hips: "Speak to me, babe. Say the good word, babe — speak to me in the native to-o-o-ongue!"; to Firpo's where as big noises (burra sahibs) we paid one rupee, seven pence, for a long refreshing John Collins. Despite war and soldiery Firpo's was elegant; before them it must have been luxurious. It seemed to be a rich, luscious diadem on the head of a starved beggar, part hotel but largely restaurant, bars, and dancing delight. Tolerantly, a good American negro pianist played to amuse us, only slightly arrogant.

Calcutta abounded with food and liquor, cinemas and servicemen, servants in spotless white, barefoot, turbanned, and the lotus life made us lustful so that we visited a brothel — my second ever — where in the reception room a syphilitic half-caste harlot lay back and indolently raised one knee to disclose that she had forgotten to put on her underclothing, a sight which nearly made me physically sick and did something to my psyche too — lust drained away in an instant, and Mowbray joined my precipitate retreat. Instead we went

151

to the cinema, to be intrigued by hours of endless music and dance geared for the naïve multitudes, but I sat in spellbound fascination at the strange rhythms and exotic tunes.

We bumped into a group of pilots from 52 Squadron, flying Dakota (DC3) transports out of Dumdum, one of Calcutta's airports, who were to prove staunch parties to a rather one-sided friendship, perhaps because we were fighting men. One of their routine runs took us to Agartala of the cigarette carton, and having by now listened insatiably to men I had met who had actually been in Burma, much of my apprehension had begun to depart. Hardly see a snake, they said, at which I brightened. Jungle isn't all that awful, which perked me up. The Nips (Japanese) are beginning to take a thrashing, at which I felt almost cheerful. Very few casualties really, and not nearly as much disease as you may have heard; I smiled merrily.

Agartala was the base for another crowd of Dakotas which dropped supplies over the thick, wet Chin Hills under escort of the Singarbil Hurricanes; within a few hours a truck arrived driven by Tommy Trimmer, a Canadian who commanded one of the Flights of No. 9 Royal Indian Air Force Squadron; he welcomed us cheerily and then we bumped along mysterious jungle tracks, through dank mangrove swamps, until we reached Singarbil in the foothills close to head-hunting Naga territory over which the Squadron operated. It was late July and the monsoon was about to break. The wet air hung like a saturated cloak enveloping the surrounding jungle, the great heat sending up daylong clouds of steam. It was like living in a Turkish bath.

The camp, some distance from the airstrip, consisted of a red dirt road, on either side of which stood bashas, bamboo bungalows, comprising the administrative buildings, messes and living accommodation. The Commanding Officer, adjutant, half a dozen pilots, and the chiefies but for one or two, were British, everybody else Indian. There was racial segregation of the messes, and latrines. Indians squat rather than sit, and for some reason preferred ours to their own, so that before use we had to wipe away their muddy footmarks. Each night, after dinner we gravitated to the Indian pilots' mess or they to ours, and we got on excellently. Most of them had been to school in England and came from high-caste families. As pilots they were brilliant rather than good: perhaps a bit too flashy. For example, they low-flew lower than anyone, and naturally there had to be occasions when they hit the ground, and that was the end of them. Among what I learnt about the Indian mentality, two facts seemed outstanding. First, it is not only legitimate but desirable to kick your immediate inferior, who kicks the man next down the line, and so on. The caste system is incredibly complex, with Brahmins, Kshatriyas, Vaisyas, Sudrahs, Pariahs, and so on. In that way there is always somebody kickable, until you reach the Untouchables, and they are beneath kicking. The second lesson was what is meant by truth. "Did you steal my wallet?" will only lead to uproar if the answer is "Yes." So the answer must be "No", because that way unpleasantness all round is avoided.

To reply "No, Sahib, sorry, Sahib," to the question "Did you clean my boots?" will only make Sahib angry. The correct answer is thus "Yes Sahib, cleaned them v-werry vwell, Sahib", which makes Sahib pleased. It is subjective truthfulness, and it is certainly philosophically arguable that it is a more sensible and therefore a more proximately absolute truth.

Campanda, one of the friendly Indian pilots, was a Parsee from Bombay, a fire-worshipper with the education and heart of a wellbred Englishman; or so I thought, until he told me how he earned his living before joining the RIAF, adding "And believe me, I was earning (some vast fortune) every month after paying all office expenses, bribes, evwerryt'ing . . ." I found the Indian mentality subtle and devious, with the Parsee closer to the western way of thinking than the Hindu or Moslem. Between the latter two groups I sensed a deep division of history as well as religion, and it seemed to me that the fires of hatred smouldered never far below the surface. Not many years later that assessment was to prove horrifyingly accurate.

The adjutant was a jolly, fat, middle-aged Lancastrian who took me to his heart, so that by the time that Molly Malone arrived back from Delhi we were buddies, and he and Molly were soon threatening to recommend me for a commission, notwithstanding my record of misbehaviour and my Father's alienness. The Englishmen other than Trimmer, who come to think of it was Canadian, were not really noteworthy except for Deal, who come to think of it was Australian and used to poop off his .38 revolver at the slightest or even no provocation. One night he was reading rather late by the light of the oil lamp in the bamboo hut which housed the half-dozen British pilots, when he was politely requested to put out his light. Without a word he pulled out his .38 and shot out the lamp. On another occasion he shot at one of the chiefies, but only flesh-wounded him. When he battered another man with fists and boots and half-killed him, he was posted. Some of the Australians I met in the RAF were extremely tough physically, but an element of kindness and gentleness was invariably combined — except in the case of Deal.

And for me also the time had once again arrived for action.

CHAPTER
EIGHT

Orientation

Trimmer led a familiarisation flight over the jungle to acquaint me with the terrain and its peculiar navigational problems and propensities; at the same time we were on the lookout for enemy targets. Flying south in our Hurricanes towards the Arakan coastal plain he suddenly dived into a jungle clearing alongside a stream, tracers flaring from his cannons. Following down I could see a group of Japanese soldiers round a camp fire, others washing in the stream, obviously a patrol resting. As Trimmer pulled clear and away I opened up, firing slap into the middle of them before pulling away. It was all so swift I could only glimpse the flitting bodies, but the shambles must have been great, for the twenty-millimetre shells of our four cannons were a mixture of semi-armour piercing, incendiary and high explosive, as well as tracer. For the first time I had killed men, dispassionately if not with pleasure. An image of the attack on that clearing, of the Japanese soldiers, resting and defenceless, has remained to trouble me to this day. They didn't have a chance.

"They would have done the same to us," Trimmer said, but after the defensive/protective role of 33 Squadron,

I had to become familiar with killing and wittingly avoiding death. Apart from that incident, the operations of 9 Squadron, Royal Indian Air Force, were of the same ilk as those of No. 33. During the several weeks I remained with them we provided fighter escort for the Agartala Dakotas over and among the Chin Hills, where at predetermined points ("Dropping Zones", or "DZ's") they parachuted or threw out supplies to the troops operating there in company with the headhunting Naga tribesmen. In previous years the monsoon had heralded a termination of air operations, but in 1944 for the first time the air war was carried on throughout its duration, thereby upsetting enemy calculations. After rendezvousing with a group of three or four Dakotas, we reported by radio, "Have found our Babies," and then accompanied them on the slow journey through interminable cloud-layers, higher and higher into the mountains until they reached the DZ, marked out in strips of white cloth which stood out boldly among the cap of dense green jungle. Often the lumbering Babies orbited in deep valleys enclosed on all sides by dank mountains and above by dense cloud, while the Hurricanes wheeled to and fro like sentries outside Buckingham Palace, alert for the attacking Japanese Zero fighters. Which never came while we were around. But only let the Babies venture abroad without Nanny and they were shot down, as sure as God made apples — on one occasion, five in the morning; we saw the smouldering remains on our next trip the same afternoon, and sighed for the men burnt alive within the wrecks.

As soon as they had discharged their cargoes and were safely on their way home the Babies dismissed us, as we carried insufficient fuel to lumber along at their slow pace the whole way back. They relied on the cloud to cover them. It was then that our own Scottish cloud-flying training came into its own, as we flew blind in tight formation down from the Chin Hills. Formation-flying consisted largely of very fine adjustments of throttle and rudder, the throttle-nut loosened to enable the most delicate movement. Easing the throttle causes deceleration, as important in handling an engined apparatus as the more familiar acceleration — something of which the skilled motorist is aware. Every movement had to be executed with utmost sensitivity, for the formation had to be very closely tucked in. Even then, because of the cloud's density, all that could be seen was wing-edge of the adjoining plane, with its red and blue roundel. The formation leader was responsible for the navigation, the other members of the formation fully occupied in maintaining precise formation by continuous minute movements of throttle and rudder. It was an effort of maximum concentration, and very eerie. The eeriness was unrelieved when breaking cloud to find ourselves sandwiched between two layers of turbulent fleece, with awe-inspiring cumulus mountains piling up tens of thousands of feet all around, while rain pounded at our tiny windscreens. Monsoon cloud had different qualities: white cloud, though turbulent, was safe; grey was distinctly unpleasant, with draughts which lifted us five thousand feet at a gasp, or violently pressed us the same distance earthwards. Brown cloud had to be avoided at all costs, and not a few aircraft which flew into it were literally ripped apart by the savage gusts it engenders. On a disastrous occasion in the Imphal Valley, only one out of a squadron of twelve Hurricanes emerged from the brown cloud they had flown into — the rest had disintegrated, their young men with them.

To break cloud above high ground is to court disaster, but our training had taught us to stay in the cloud well above ground level until there could be no doubt that one was safely over the sea. Then the cloud base was penetrated, and the formation could turn back towards land, flying in safety beneath the dense layers above them. It was a hazardous business.

We flew as many as four sorties a day, each with half-a-dozen aircraft. When not flying, the day was spent hanging about the flight tent in a clearing between the runway and the jungle, drinking prodigious quantities of pressed limes and awaiting flying orders. The runway consisted of skeletonised metal planking laid on top of absorbent tarred felt, which provided a dry landing under the wettest of conditions, though clanking alarmingly as an aircraft touched down. It was known as "Sommerfeld tracking". One spectacularly loud clank was provided by Butler, a sergeant-pilot, who ignored the red Very light fired across his bows and landed without having lowered his undercarriage, slithering along the metal planks, not on the belly of his Hurricane but on the long-range fuel tanks attached to the underside of his wings. The friction of metal against metal at ninety

159

miles an hour sent up showers of sparks, which should have ignited the fuel tanks, blowing the plane and him sky high. But being charmed, like the rest of us, he got away with it. Of course, we did not think of dying; the other chap might, probably would, sometimes did, but it never happened to oneself, always the other poor bastard. For a magical voice whispered in our enchanted ears, "Young man — you'll never die!" It is only when that voice falls silent that the superb confidence of youth is known to have passed, and one is wiser, if sadder.

During each hot steamy monsoon day, when the sun scorched intensely above layers of thick cloud and occasionally blasted a way through, the slightest movement induced a stream of sweat from every pore. The chafing of parachute-straps and safety-harness did little to assuage the impact of "prickly heat", a red rash which covered every man's back with screaming itchiness, relieved only by allowing the evening instalment of monsoon deluge to soak onto the bare skin. The monsoon was utterly predictable and — brown cloud apart — devoid of any real malice. Apart from starting on a predetermined day in August and finishing similarly in November, it also had regular diurnal habits, which we put to use. By five-thirty in the afternoon we would be drinking appalling locally-brewed gin in the mess, waiting for the reliable weather forecast due fifteen minutes later, and on the dot it arrived — a sudden strong puff of cool wind blown in through the open bamboo door. We rushed to our bashas, tearing off our clothes as we went, chucked

160

them untidily on the verandah then stood out in the open, naked, to bathe in the unbelievable wall of solid sheet rain which was the start of the day's serious instalment of warm monsoon. Although lasting barely ten minutes, the precipitation was a couple of days' volume by home standards. The deluge provided not only the day's shower bath but, more importantly, relief from the maddening itch of prickly heat. Slackening to a heavy shower, it continued for an hour while we towelled dry, then the cloud passed to leave a clear hot evening, orchestrated by crickets, bullfrogs and termites, and jewelled with rich glowing insects disporting among the soaking foliage all around us.

At night, lying on a charpoy, a rough Indian bed of stout timbers laced with thick sisal ropes to provide a mattress base, the tattooing of termites was persistent enough to interrupt sleep. With insatiable appetite and little discrimination, slowly but steadily they ate away the plaited walls and thatched roofs of the bamboo bungalows which housed us, and nothing could stop them. It was sad to reflect that they were not even enjoying their xylophagous feasting, but merely collecting food to spew out to the faceless community which was their termitary. As well as that tyranny, they had other enemies, such as the tawny toad who was quickly on the scene one stifling day when, after kicking at an old hat lying on the ground, its crown flew away to reveal a small army of ugly fat white ants feeding off the rim. Startled by the sudden daylight they marched round and round in a worried unthinking circle while the toad, stationed some inches outside their perimeter, shot forward rhythmically on his long hind legs to pick off the anxious army one by one until he was gorged.

The large red "warrior" ants had a more sinister enemy, a horned beetle who dug inverted conical pits along the ants' favourite runs in the right angle where verandah floor and bungalow walls met. The pits were perhaps five inches wide at ground level, tapering to a point some six inches down, below which the beetle lurked invisibly beneath the cone's bottom. Woe betide the ant, however large and strong, who failed to give the innocent-looking pits a wide berth, for the powdery earth walls of the pit quickly precipitated him to its bottom, where the invisible predator seized and dragged him under. Fascinated, we watched scores of fights as warriors struggled desperately to escape, but I only ever saw one which did. A powerful warrior might break the grip of the strong jaws holding his legs and scramble desperately up the side of the trap towards freedom, but the earth had been so finely dug as to be sand-like and, unable to afford his limbs a secure purchase, caused him to tumble down yet again to his waiting doom. Or if he should appear to be making good his escape, the invisible foe had only to dig a fraction deeper for the surface of the pit's walls to slide away down to the nadir, carrying the hapless warrior with them. The fight could go on as long as twenty minutes.

But far and away the most important insects in or lives were malarial mosquitoes, against whom we endured the suffocation of nets strung around our charpoys. It did not however seem difficult for an artful one or two to sneak in as we retired, which required the momentary raising of the net, and frantic slapping became the order of the night to dispatch the enemy feeding off our blood. I was never so parsimonious as to begrudge them a little of mine, but bridled at their coldly clinical collection methods, which consisted of pricking the skin and inserting a quantity of anti-clotting chemical before commencing sucking operations. The irritation of the chemical only became felt after their grossly distended bellies had been filled and they had withdrawn to digest the feast, but occasionally a prompt smack in the direction of the itch resulted in one's blood, complete with exploded mosquito, being spread over one's skin. If on the other hand the insect withdrew smartly enough, a wild chase round the inside of the net ensued in the darkness, the direction of attack being guided by the frantic whine of the tiny vibrating wings. Malaria was rife, and my turn eventually arrived when for a week or so I lay in a stupefying fever, alternating between semi-delirious singing (to cheer myself up, I thought) and tolerable equanimity, while eyeballs and joints ached in fierce accord. That was just before the introduction of mepacrine, a highly effective anti-malaria drug which thereafter was part of our daily ingestion, and which turned us bright yellow.

The supply drops enabled the Army's counter-offensive against the Japanese to continue unexpected throughout the monsoon season so that, wrong-footed, the enemy was forced out of the hills down into the Arakan coastal plane. We moved to Hathazari, near the port of Chittagong, and from there carried out strikes and offensive patrols down the Arakan Coast and on the offshore islands of Ramree and Akyab, in the course of which many thousands of Japanese were killed and their transports destroyed by our cannon. I was surprised at the ease with which I adjusted to my new "work" — a change of role to offensive/aggressive. I realised why I enjoyed it. Natural self-protectiveness gives rise to defensive reactions associated with running away, though in our case we had simply stayed and become bored. On the other hand, deliberately to go out and attack, to seek and destroy, promotes overdoses of adrenalin, which in turn produces the same sense of pleasure as physical effort, both at the time of the effort and afterwards.

The Navy was by now island-hopping, taking the chain just off the Arakan coast, our daily targets always slightly further south, and there was no doubt that the enemy was in retreat. Contained at Imphal, they had been pushed back from their climatic position at India's very threshold, as the tide of battle turned for what was to be the last time.

Hathazari, close to the sea and free of the jungle's stranglehold, contrasted pleasantly with the steam and heat of Singarbil. Housed again in bamboo bashas, we enjoyed a servant staff augmented by local labour, men and boys whose features were broad, a different race from the fine-nosed Indians; they are in fact Polynesian, like most races south-east of India. Beni, a silent twelve-year-old, attached himself to me and for the equivalent of a few pence a day catered for my domestic requirements — early morning tea, bed-making, laying out clothes, and attending to their laundering and pressing. Being waited on hand and foot was one of the distinctions between operational service in this zone of the Far East and the Western Desert; a benefit of Empire, or perhaps merely a manifestation of the caste system.

There was a hill at one end of the runway, a rendezvous for a pack of evil-looking vultures who we thought were waiting for our blood, most reprehensible among them the "kings", with bald crimson heads and necks. They led the onslaught on the pack's prey, disembowelling the carcase through its natural orifices; it is to that interstitial surgery that their featherless red heads are attributed. Campanda, the Parsee, explained the usefulness of vultures in a tropical climate, where the heat renders corpses rotten in a day. "It is v-werry hygienic," he said, and indeed Parsees rely on the vulture to dispose of the flesh of their dead, whose bodies are placed on bleached funeral towers for that purpose. Not much later he crashed into the jungle and died an airman's death. I hoped the vultures found him. Adjunctive to the Hathazari vultures were yowling hyenas, craven creatures which slunk nightly round the camp's outskirts. Even hunger does not make them bold. Moving in packs they feast on what others have killed, waiting for the original predator to sate itself before moving in for their turn. They are cleaners-up.

Our Arakan offensive was paralleled across the far side of the mountain range where lay the Kabaw Valley,

165

beyond which again, some hundreds of miles from where we were operating, lay Siam, the general direction of the Japanese retreat. Our first objective was to push them across into the Kabaw Valley and at the same time to break out from Imphal at its northern end, in a unified beat eastwards and south. On alternate days we operated from an airfield at Cox's Bazaar; there was very little to see of the bazaar itself, one of the last trading posts before the jungle imposed its impenetrable authority. Sensibly, the traders had long since left for safer parts. Here I developed a liking for the dark, winding Burmese cheroot which slowly replaced the forty-odd cigarettes I had smoked daily since joining up. In inevitable course the cheroots led to the somewhat smoother Havanas which were to become part of my middle-aged comfort.

Both the Air Officer Commanding and the Group Captain in charge of the Wing to which No. 9 Indian Squadron belonged, were regular and enthusiastic visitors, seldom standing on ceremony; their lively interest and friendliness created an excellent atmosphere. It was good to feel that there was someone who knew and appreciated our warlike efforts.

Heedless of my warnings, Molly Malone had recommended me for a commission, and first the Group Captain and then the AOC interviewed me at Hathazari. The former asked: "If you're flying from Cox's tomorrow, shall we do a sortie together?" As he and I had previously carried out several destructive strikes together, that penetrating interview came to a swift and amicable conclusion. The AOC was longer-winded. He was a thoroughly pleasant regular officer, but extremely dim-witted. "Look here," he snapped, addressing me by my Christian name as he was accustomed to do, "I don't understand this. How the devil can you be fighting in the British forces when your father is an enemy alien!"

"His nationality is just a technical accident, Sir" I explained soothingly. "I'm British."

Testily, "Can't see how you can be, dammit. Still, you've got away with it for long enough, I suppose I can recommend you . . . Been flying today?"

"This afternoon, Sir."

"How d'ye get on?"

"We knocked out a few tanks and quite a few personnel."

"Good show! Press on! We've got the Nips on the run."

We had indeed, and we were knocking hell out of them if they showed themselves during daylight, smashing up their tanks, lorries, and troops. They had to lie hidden, and make their way over to the Kabaw Valley under cover of darkness. Our effort came to a lull, and I took the opportunity to spend a few days in Calcutta where I went to the races, which as far as my untutored eye could tell were completely crooked; rode in the comfortably rocking horse-drawn gharries; over-indulged at Firpo's; and got into trouble with a pyard, one of the skinny, wild, rabid dogs which roam Calcutta's streets. It was after a particularly good lunch. I teetered out of Firpo's into the dazzling early afternoon sunlight and inadvertently trod on the wretched creature. My first awareness of the situation was when I realised that somebody or something had suddenly fixed a very tight clamp round the lower part of my left leg, and even in my condition it did not take long to realise that the mangy cur slinking away had sunk its fangs into me. I fondly imagined that having got round the corner it would hiccough loudly thrice, roll over on its back with its legs in the air and expire, reeking of gin. In the taxi to the military hospital I examined my wounds, quite impressive considering that the animal had bitten once only; we had been made familiar with the terrors of rabies, or hypochondria, and the necessity for prompt counter-action. My efforts to dissuade the doctor from cauterisation were brusquely brushed aside and I participated in the strange sensation of watching my own flesh being burnt under my nose, as a piece of caustic on the end of a wire was ritually stirred round inside the two bites. I was all ready to yell my head off, but for all the sizzle, smoke and stench of burning flesh there was no pain at all. Enormous quantities of liquid serum were then pushed under the loose skin near my navel, and I was sent away with a box of twenty-eight large phials for the Squadron doctor to inject twice daily.

"But I'm on leave and won't be back with my unit for another four days."

That produced a second box containing a monster sized hypodermic syringe and a set of do-it-yourself instructions.

"Twice a day, remember, subcutaneously, in the vicinity of the navel." He had a Scots accent.

Somebody organised a two-day visit to Colombo, twelve hundred and fifty miles south, as he knew some Wrens there. Complete with my boxes we flew on one of 52 Squadron's daily mail runs to Ratmalana, staying at the Aircrew Club where the Wrens came to a dance. Although by now nearly twenty-four, I had not even begun to acquire the modicum of suavity, necessary for success when there's a lot of competition around, but one of the Wrens took pity on me and even agreed to see me the next day. We sunbathed on the beach at Mount Lavinia, an idyllic Polynesian-type beach whose scalding sands were subdued to seaward by roaring surf and to landward by pineapple-palms bending their fronds in shady benediction, while local girls, swathed in saris, plied us with peeled pineapples at tuppence a go. We were not even unduly disturbed by the nationalist-minded Sinhalese boys who occasionally chucked large stones at us. Was not all of mankind brothers? Then to enhance the romance there were freshwater showers, and tea on the sweet-smelling lawn of the hotel on the promontory alongside. Night fell, and the blue-black sky backclothed a million stars brighter than ever I had seen, while the surf pounded and hissed, and the warm air engulfed us. It was paradise itself, and contrasted very pleasingly with Arakan life. Romance was undoubtedly in that soft air.

In the town I suffered for the rickshaw boys, sweat-sodden through pulling their hearts out, though without our patronage perhaps they would have suffered still more. There was a proud caste of half-breeds, the Burghers, of Dutch-Sinhalese descent, wealthy and with luscious but untouchable daughters. They seemed more dignified than Calcutta's Anglo-Indians, innocent offspring of Europeans who spurned and Indians who ostracised them. The real drawback to the romance was my twice-daily self-injection of the contents of one of those gigantic phials into my midriff, followed by rubbing down the sizeable bulge thereby created. The jokiness of it was already beginning to evaporate.

Calcutta saw me briefly on my way back to Hathazari, where I handed my boxes to the Medical Officer. By now my belly was sore with hypodermic pricking, and still there were over a dozen injections to endure. We ran out of available places where the needle had not previously been inserted and had to start a second time round over already-used territory, so that I flinched at the very thought of my twice-daily visits.

Late, we moved south to Ramu in pursuit of the Japanese.

CHAPTER
NINE

Death Valley

Molly was as good as his word, and three days before Christmas 1944, I was posted to Number 11 Squadron, RAF, flying Hurricanes at Tamu, at the northernmost end of the Kabaw Valley — Death Valley, as it was known because of its malarial reputation; the Squadron had just moved there from Imphal, where the Battle of Kohima had turned the tide finally against the Japanese. There, allegedly, was coined the expression: "The impossible we do at once — miracles take a little longer!"

I made a bad start on the new outfit. As the Dakota mail-plane came to a halt in the jungle clearing which constituted RAF Station, Tamu, I was welcomed by a group of the pilots and we introduced ourselves. "Is there anyone who can carry my bags?" I asked, in all innocence assuming that there would be bearers, attached in large numbers to the Indian Air Force squadrons. A little curtly, the unequivocal answer came, "We carry our own gear." Explanations would have taken too long, so that was one I had simply to live down over the ensuing months. It must have sounded too high and mighty for words, and totally out of character with the RAF, where vainglory is tolerated from no man, however distinguished, however bemedalled, however lofty his rank.

Until a few days earlier Tamu had been a Japanese base, and when evacuated its bamboo huts were pushed flat by bulldozers, then the site intensively sprayed from the air with DDT, effectively destroying the insect life and along with it a lot of actual and potential disease. The bulldozers, an important part of the advancing Fourteenth Army's equipment, had cleared a strip big enough to take the Dakotas which transported the Squadron's technical and personal equipment and the two hundred-odd ground staff, with an auxiliary small strip for use by the Auster ambulance aircraft which flew out the wounded — the burra strip and the kutcha strip. The debris of the former camp was burnt, including articles of clothing and other utility used by the Korean "comfort-girls" who followed wherever the enemy army went, and the place was a paragon of hygiene.

The CO, a lean, dark, hard-bitten New Zealander known as the Black Prince, had spent some time with Wingate's Chindits campaigning deep in the jungle, and was currently awaiting repatriation. That saturnine character's welcoming speech consisted of a query why, with all the experience disclosed by my pilot's logbook, I had not been commissioned and, after learning that I had been recommended, of a cursory statement that now I was on his squadron he would stop that little nonsense until he was satisfied about my fitnesss to be an officer. Not an altogether encouraging reception.

A Christmas party held there al fresco in the jungle sunshine afforded officers and senior NCOs the Saturnalian opportunity of serving dinner to the airmen, and everybody was extremely cheerful — a different atmosphere from that which too often pervaded us in the desert, largely because here there was an unaccustomed adequacy of liquor. The food, though more varied, was as terrible, with weird concoctions such as dehydrated mutton (which looked remarkably like sheep's droppings and tasted correspondingly sinister), dehydrated potato, and the like. We lived in tents, six to a hundred-and-fifty-pounder, designed to house two in comfort. So that we could all get under some sort of cover we raised the short vertical walls towards the horizontal, with the result that we were unprotected from the cold, and when rain drove, from that also. Although the monsoon was well over, it nevertheless rained a great deal and nights were distinctly cool; normal evening attire was the same khaki worn in the UK. When we joked about the rheumatism we'd have if we lived to tell the tale, I thought of my Mother's exhortations to remember at all times to ensure that my underclothes were aired thoroughly. But then, in the rare letters which reached me, she was still enjoining me not to fly too fast, and to stay nice and near the ground. During the day the temperature stayed at about eighty-five, a hot summer's day at home.

The pilots, mostly British, though with the usual sprinkling of colonials, included a highly articulate Scots Home Ruler who introduced me not only to the

173

splinter group idea but also to the second movement of Beethoven's Seventh Symphony, which we sang contrapuntally and endlessly; and Aussies from places with outlandish names such as Wagga-Wagga, always good for a laugh. Other musical activities included my participation with Eddie Carlton in a duet — a rendering of *The Waiter and the Porter and the Upstairs Maid*, with one or two snazzy dance steps thrown in. He strongly resembled Hoagy Carmichael in appearance and perhaps for that reason became my "Oppo", or closest friend. Also I wrote the lyric for one of his own songs, which he called "Yesterday's Dream." Another of our Scots, who left the Squadron not long after I had joined, and whom I was not to see again until a chance encounter at a Hampshire point-to-point exactly twenty years later, was reputed to have been on patrol over the Imphal Valley when ground control informed him of twenty-plus Jap Zero fighters at ground level below him. Now the Zero could walk rings round the decrepit old Hurricanes, and upon recipt of the information Jock looked down and allegedly, if discreetly, replied: "So there are, so there are," before returning smartly to base.

We flew both day and night. During the day we foraged far afield with long-range fuel tanks slung beneath the wings of the Hurricanes, attacking anything and everything that moved, for the Japs, now in desperate straits, were commandeering sampans and even bullock-carts to evacuate men and equipment south and east towards Siam. At night, by moonlight, we frequently carried five-hundred-pound high-explosive bombs, one under each wing, with which we monotonously blasted the railhead at a place whose name was unpronounceable, but which we phoneticised into "Pink Gin." Night-flying was still eerie and unnatural. Navigation was elementary, a course laid off on a map, repeated on the compass, visual recognition of the unmistakeable king-size rivers which snake through Burma, the silver glitter of the railway line leading to Pink Gin, and for the return journey a range of hills between the Chindwin River and Tamu which included a dromedary-hump affair; provided one flew through the declivity at the correct angle, the flarepath was likely to be there waiting for you. Not, however, on one occasion when a Jap bomber had been whining around a few minutes before the arrival of one of the night-flyers and we'd had to extinguish the paraffin-fed gooseneck flares. There wasn't time to relight them after the intruder had shoved off, and hastily we rushed out every available motor vehicle, spacing them alongside the runway with headlights blazing, to provide a makeshift flarepath, for the Hurricanes could not carry enough fuel to go into a prolonged orbit while the flares were relit.

Night-flying was uncanny, and I always had a strong feeling that we should have been in bed, not tearing round the skies under that insane moon. I suppose a psychiatrist would have leapt unerringly to some erudite diagnosis were I then to have disclosed my secret correlation of "monsoon" with "moon-sun". Just an example of jungle-happiness. Perhaps an affinity with the moon explains why Pilkington, one of the sergeant-pilots, returned from a night-trip to slow-roll his Hurricane, long-range tanks and all, five hundred feet above the strip, while we watched in amazement as the lights on his wing-tips cartwheeled; at that height the manoeuvre is not without danger in daylight, and without long-range tanks, and it is doubtful whether his feat has ever been accomplished, before or since. He was a fearless and excellent pilot.

The Intelligence Officer, Mike Bolton, known as the Spy, not only briefed but also on our return debriefed us, waiting in his cosy tent with a certain cup of hot tea to interrogate us about the trip, and his welcome was a distinct compensation for what were undoubtedly the perils and discomforts of night operations. Then before retiring we might play our favourite record on the battered old gramophone we cherished — the Mills Brothers singing *The Moonlight's There Tonight Along the Wabash*, our private rendering of which, sung lustily and in sublime harmony especially on non-flying nights, substituted "Chindwin" for "Wabash."

In addition to "ghoolie-chits" similar to those carried in the desert, but in four different languages of the vicinity, we carried in a neat package fitting a pocket in the leg of our jungle-green trousers an assortment of accessories designed to provide a chance of survival should we find ourselves parted from our Hurricanes — the traditional fifty pounds worth of silver coins; miniature compass secretable within the body; a map printed on silk which could be used as handkerchief, scarf or bandage; a tiny, waterproof box of matches; a slim steel gadget measuring two inches by one comprising razor blade, burning glass and horses' hoof device all in one; a fishing line complete with hook; a pack of condensed chocolate to provide several days' nourishment; and a quantity of benzedrine pills which would obviate the need for sleep for up to seventy-two hours of what could of course be a vital period of one's life. And we wore and carried as basic equipment the wherewithal to survive the jungle — longsleeved dark green shirts, long green drill trousers gaitered to obstruct access to the multitudinous insects intent to feed off one; marching boots; and an armoury, slung from a webbing belt, consisting of the usual .38 Smith & Wesson revolver with a pouchful of ammunition, a Ghurka kukri — a two-foot-long knife with a cruel curved blade of tempered steel, one swipe with which could decapitate a man; a fierce Commando dagger for silent stabbing; and the standard Service penknife complete with two blades and the inescapable gadget for getting stones out of horses' hooves.

The only man you could reasonably expect to kill with the .38 was yourself, really its prime function should one unhappily be about to fall into Japanese hands. For the enemy had officially announced that all Allied airmen captured by the Imperial Nipponese Forces would be summarily executed by the sword, and wide publicity was given to a notorious photograph of a wretched American flying-man kneeling on the ground, hands tied behind his back, head hanging forward, while a Jap soldier swung a mighty sword down towards his miserable outstretched neck. Propaganda or no, that picture made quite an impression and played no small part in incensing us to strike repeated, angered blows for what we had by now stopped calling Churchillian dictatorship. We were stirred into a deep hatred of the Japanese. They were still convinced that they were divinely guided. They fought to the death, believing too that the flag they wrapped round their midriff would protect them. They lost over two hundred and forty thousand dead in the Burma retreat, only a literal handful being taken prisoner. The story went round that six prisoners had actually been taken, guarded by a couple of Ghurkas; when the British Intelligence Officer turned up to interrogate the prisoners he noticed that the Ghurkas were holding their kukris, and remarked that he had thought their tradition was never to draw them from their scabbards without also drawing blood. "Ask prisoners to nod heads," replied one of the Ghurkas, "and see what happens."

Daytime flying was hot as hell, the humidity intense, and as soon as the Spy had released us we ran along jungle tracks between tall elephant grass to a swift, limpid stream which flowed over cool stones and was shaded from the sun by lofty overhanging trees, so that its water was ice-cold. A crude log dam created a deep pool into which we dived, gasping at the chilling impact of the *chaung*. The insects might have been subjugated in the immediate proximity of the airstrip, but down by the *chaung* they bred fervently, and leeches often attached themselves to our nude bodies, to grow fat on our blood. Once discovered, sprinkled salt encouraged their speedy, if bloated, departure, but you could lose a dangerous quantity of blood should half-a-dozen of them remain undetected overnight, as occasionally happened. Another horror was the tick, a tiny insect with steel claws which he embedded in your flesh together with his head, to make him dislodgeable while he ate you. Although warned never to leave clothing near any foliage, foolishly I hung mine on a bush before plunging into the *chaung* and unbeknown to me my underclothing harboured a sinister enemy. The tick duly embedded itself in an embarrassingly intimate part of my body, undiscovered until a day later by when I was in considerable swollen discomfort. Unavailingly I tried to eradicate my gratuitous satellite with liberal quantities of salt, then with no small reluctance by the application of heat — to be accurate, I had to be held down while somebody else did the applying. The tick seemed merely to burrow deeper, until the MO, blessed man of science, suffocated the tiny brute with a smelly oily substance, then excised him utterly with a sharp scalpel, leaving me scarred for life. The only more unpleasant accident of that nature which can be imagined occurred a little later when a certain Group Captain, in preparation for a cool refreshing swim in the Irrawaddy, donned his bathing trunks without having taken the customary precaution of shaking them out. Unfortunately they harboured a scorpion, and the wretched Groupie was very ill in hospital for three months; one can only hope that his recovery was total. But there was a lesson in it, namely that bathing trunks are not a suitable item of military clothing. Certainly we never swam except nude.

But it was not long afterwards that I came near to wrecking totally my own future when constructing makeshift shelving from one of the tough cardboard boxes in which the fins of our bombs were delivered. The adopted method, using the lethal Commando dagger, comprised cutting three slots in the face of the box, two vertical with a horizontal one joining them across the top, then bending back the flap thus created to wedge itself, and thereby form a useful shelf; two or three shelves could be carved out of one box, providing a highly utilitarian item of furniture. Unluckily, my dagger slipped on the shiny surface, and as I happened to be gripping the box between my knees, inflicted a grievous wound which bled profusely. Once again I had to visit the MO's tent, concerned that I might be bleeding to death, or at least be in danger of losing my most valuable appendage. For the next two weeks I sported a tiny bandage, neatly tied with a bow. In view of the total absence of privacy in the conduct of our more natural everyday affairs, I was accused of ostentation.

My disaster compared minimally with the accident which befell Medway, a thin narcissist who daily wiled away the spare hours in front of a steel mirror hung on the guyropes outside his tent, oiling and combing his wavy black locks and sleeking a pencil-thin moustache. Peacefully ensconced on one of the line of six wooden thrones placed over the pit dug as a first chore upon making camp, he was smoking a calm, thoughtful cigarette. Forgetful of the fact that the pit was kept sanitary by liberal daily application of used engine-oil, he tossed his fag-end down between his knees where it ignited the rising vapours. These exploded violently, blowing him off his seat and removing most of the hair from his body, though sparing one eyebrow, one half of the dapper moustache, and some of the glossy waves. The steel mirror had its face turned to the canvas, and Medway departed on prolonged sick leave.

My commission arrived with the rations early in January 1945, backdated a few months. I had been "commissioned in the field," a bullshit term. Who knows what it is like being "in the field" — campaigning — who hasn't actually done it? and they don't talk about it. On the contrary, they occlude, so as not to remember the awful discomforts and privations, as one does with a great pain. However, I was a Pilot Officer and became entitled to use the Officers' Mess, just another tent. The same afternoon there was an enthusiastic rugger match on the *kutcha* (light aircraft) strip, when the Squadron played the Wing — the administrative organisation whose function was to impel the squadrons ever forward. One of their team, a handsome lad who looked only a little older than I, repeatedly infringed by hanging on to the ball after being tackled; when, despite my reading him the Riot Act, he persisted, I took the first opportunity of engaging him in the sort of admonitory set-to which rugger-players will understand. The same evening, somewhat self-consciously entering the Officers' Mess for the first time, I sat in a quiet corner on a camp-stool, drinking and yarning to pass the evening with some of the dozen or so denizens.

"Ah, here's the new Group Captain," announced Eastman, a Flight Lieutenant who was acting as Commanding Officer whilst the Black Prince's replacement was awaited, and went over to greet the newly-arrived visitor. Horror of horrors! it was the good-looking lad of the rugger field. Hapless me — well, bang goes my commisssion the same day I got it, I thought glumly; at least, it would set up a new record of sorts, and was not altogether out of character. Keeping my head well buried in the tent wall I concentrated hard on my tankard, aiming at invisibility. To no avail. Eastman approached the ostrich.

"The new Groupie would like to meet you," he said.

It was like having a tooth out, and I groaned inwardly. What possible subterfuge was available? I could be sick, quite easily, and dash past him out of the tent. Or just crawl under the nearest canvas wall, make a beeline for the jungle, and live off the land for a time, like the Japs did. I could join their side. I might even think up a military secret or two for them. My head was hot and filled with awful vapours as I crawled reluctantly to the spot where the handsome lad stood, ring upon ring of office emblazoned on either epaulette. As we were introduced, he was gazing at me, I thought sardonically, probably sadistically as well.

"Sir," I gulped miserably, and waited for it.

"Enjoy the rugger this afternoon?" he enquired tenderly.

No words came, so I tried to nod the gaseous balloon attached to the end of my neck.

"You're a keen player, I gather?" he continued "know all the rules and that?"

Again the wretched balloon wobbled an incoherent answer.

"Quite a good game, I thought," he added, reminiscently.

"Sir," uttered the hot bubble.

He hadn't finished; he was enjoying himself; he was going to give me some more, a lot more. By then I had all but fainted away with unhappiness.

"I said 'What would you like to drink?'" he repeated. Close to hysteria I squeaked for gin, and as he put me at my ease I appreciated what a god of a marvellous lad he really wonderfully was and I babbled away non-stop in my relief until he too began to feel the strain of the interview and departed, perhaps a little precipitately.

Other notable visitors were the same Air Commodore who had interviewed me for my commission, except that like me he too had moved up one and was now an Air Vice Marshal; and the Supremo, Lord Louis Mountbatten, inordinately handsome and always immaculately turned out in godlike white. Being something of a psychologist he was beloved of the rank and file, whom he used to inform of future happenings and what their part in it was to be. His gambit was to order the men to break ranks and gather round him, his conclusion to invite them to tackle him personally with any problems they might have.

"Me and me brother want to join the commandos," called out one of the Braker twins, and Lord Louis actually fixed it for them. The twins were anyway in the habit of going off into the jungle with a rifle apiece hunting Japs, and must have been very successful as commandos. I used to think that Supremo might be a tidy way of saying "Supreme Allied Commander" but it sounded like ice-cream, which was frustrating. I considered the man a great bullshitter, and in this I was by no means alone.

Towards the end of January 1945 we struck camp, and the Dakotas airlifted everything except the pilots and their Hurricanes down Death Valley to Kan, where the bulldozers had cleared two strips, as at Tamu, and in no time the tents were pitched round the edge of the clearing as we settled in to our new home. Abandoning night-flying we operated exclusively as a ground-attack squadron, dive-bombing enemy positions before following up with strafing runs. We were so close to the Japanese positions that we had to execute a steep climbing turn on take-off in order to gain adequate height before attacking. From take-off to landing took less than twenty minutes, and thanks to impeccable servicing by the ground crews we were able to keep up non-stop pressure throughout the day. By now, as a result of pilot postings home, I was acting as Flight Commander of "A" Flight, and after we had been briefed it fell on me to lead its six aircraft, pair by pair joining up into a wide battle formation of three sections as we climbed to gain the five thousand feet from which we dived on the enemy. Getting those ancient Hurricanes off the ground with a five-hundred-pound bomb under each wing was not always easy, nor was it at all difficult to obey Mother's injunction not to fly too fast.

Daytime navigation consisted of map-reading along a previously pencilled line on the map, then correcting for drift by constantly pinpointing one's position over the ground. Knowing airspeed and compass bearing from one's instruments, and the mileage covered over the ground, it was not difficult to gauge the speed and direction of the wind, and by use of the clock to mapread oneself anywhere; a little later we were to range hundreds of miles to and from base without any other navigational aid. As we approached the bomb-line, which divided the opposing forces, the leader dipped a wing to indicate the selected direction for the other five pilots to position their aircraft in echelon; this was determined by geographical appraisal. The five stacked up staggered back from the leading Hurricane, at the same time depressing switches which fused and armed the bombs; and they illuminated the gunsights by which the bombs were aimed. Turning steadily, and keeping the target in sight below his wingtip, the leader with his five aircraft still in echelon behind and above him arrived back at the target but facing back the way we had come; then rolling on to our backs, one by one, we dived steeply on to a point short of the target. By the half-roll from, so to speak, the wrong direction, we in fact dived away from our own lines towards the enemy, so that a miss-hit landed in enemy territory, the tendency being to overshoot the target rather than the reverse. At two thousand feet one eased out of the dive at upwards of three hundred and twenty miles an hour and, at the moment the target disappeared under the aircraft's nose, jabbed savagely at the bomb-release button on top of the throttle lever with a "Take that, you bastards!", wheeling away in a tight diving turn to escape the blast of our own bombs and make ourselves difficult to hit.

By the time the leader's bombs exploded in the target area, the rest of the formation had dropped theirs and were wheeling away behind him, the last man being responsible for looking over his shoulder to see the results of the attack, before announcing, "White Two, off target". Strafing-runs, conducted from slightly different directions, pounded the target, often a seething inferno, with clouds of twenty-millimetre shells, as we skidded the aircraft violently on the run-in to make ourselves a difficult target for anti-aircraft fire, before breaking away violently after the attack, hugging the ground. A few moments later a second strafing run, followed by a third — the last often a dummy run, when by prearrangement we held our fire though at the same time encouraging the enemy (excluded from the secret) to keep their heads down, enabling our troops to assault the position with reduced opposition. I have never been at the end of one of those dive-bombing and strafing raids and would hate to be. Our aggressiveness and sense of destruction increased day by day, as our bombing became increasingly accurate, and on our return from many of the trips we were welcomed by congratulatory wireless signals, known as "strawberries".

On the way back to base we resumed the loose battle formation of three sections until the strip came in sight some miles ahead, when a waggle of the leader's wings indicated that it was time to tighten up into the bullshit battle formation in which we dived low over the airfield, the leading section on the left, the others on its right — a show for the ground crew. Up we pulled, for the leader to break away peeling off to his left, followed by the others at forty-second intervals until the formation was strung out equidistantly around the circuit. The leader split-arsed on to the left-hand side of the strip, his Number Two to the right, then the others left then right until all were swiftly down, in under a minute, taxied in and switched off within another. We sat limply in our cockpits awhile, before climbing out to report to the waiting Spy, weary-eyed and stiff after even a short trip, so intense were the strain and concentration — more on the landing than when we were being shot at by the enemy! Perhaps the anticlimax of being safely "home" was more exhausting than the routine risking of one's life, for to that we had long since become accustomed.

I was temporarily entrusted with the job of Squadron Adjutant, a fulltime administrative post which had unexpectedly fallen vacant, and which somebody had to undertake in order to keep the airscrews turning until the new adjutant turned up. As the post seemed to demand little beyond signing receipts for documents from various headquarters it did not interfere with my flying activities. I observed with no small interest that I was being sent receipts for my receipts, with which were enclosed chits requesting my acknowledgement of receipt of the receipt for my receipt. I suspected there was something amiss with the way I was doing the job, but perhaps headquarters included a tidy division (perhaps of the despised combat-weary) whose function was to ensure an adequate flow of receipts, thus building up not only a mighty filing system but also what was called, I learnt, an "establishment". That meant that if, for example, you were a Squadron Leader (Air Force ranks are common to flying and nonflying men alike) and were after a bit of promotion, you set about building up a case to demonstrate that the amount and importance of paperwork undertaken by your little lot merited at least Wing Commander status (the next rank up, of course with increased pay) or better still, that of Group Captain, which meant a still further ring round your sleeve and still better pay. Naturally reluctant to stimie the game, I entered into it wholeheartedly during my brief tenure of office, and the flow of receipts for receipts for receipts gained full spate. Nowadays the technique is part of what is called Parkinsonia, and is to be found everywhere, not just in the Air Force.

CHAPTER
TEN

Apotheosis

The Japanese were pulling away southwards to regroup and, their motor transport blown to pieces by our cannon, took to the rivers, travelling at night and hiding their vessels in the naturally camouflaged chaungs and creeks by day. Concentrating on the destruction of every manner of vessel — sampans, barges, motor boats, river steamers — whatever we spotted was attacked with cannon-fire and sunk. Increasingly the enemy abandoned their heavy anti-aircraft weapons, until the maximum response they could muster to our onslaught was from nothing of larger calibre than forty-five millimetre cannon, the effects of which were comfortably avoided by flying a few feet above ground level, down to which they could not depress. But let us only soar a hundred feet and magically there appeared the silent black puffs whose explosions rocked the careless Hurricanes and pierced their fabric. "Get down, Junior!" I yelled over the radio at Evershed, a fresh pink nineteen-year old just out from Blighty, and flying as my Number Two, as he drifted happily along, to all appearances oblivious of the evil black shellbursts pocking the blue sky around him. At the ripe age of twenty-four I treated that lad as if he were my own son, though I needn't have worried — his life was charmed. Regularly the Hurricanes were hit by small arms and machine-gun fire, and it was even rumoured that the Burmese were throwing stones and firing arrows at us. Eastman was shot down thrice on successive trips, twice in the snake-infested area of Meiktila, but each time contrived to find his way back to an unrestrained welcome. He had used up more than a fair share of lives and we were rapidly running out of planes on his account. The gremlins were also hard at it and the Squadron was down to five serviceable aircraft, less than a quarter of its operational strength.

At Pakokku the Japanese were holding out against all the Army's efforts to dislodge them, until our repeated dive-bombing and strafing strikes proved irresistible, and once again we struck camp and moved south down the Kabaw Valley to the next strip carved out of the reluctant jungle by the Engineers' bulldozers — at Sinthe, where we were to spend the ensuing three months, and experience events which constituted the veritable apotheosis of Number XI Squadron's Burma campaign, perhaps of its fighting history. First and foremost occurred the liquidation of the treasured moustache which had been my close and constant companion since 1941, symbol of the confidence of youthful manhood, but which now accepted its own sacrifice as a small token towards rejuvenating an ageing fighter-bomber pilot already known to the younger pilots as "Grandpa". I was after all only eight or nine months short of a quarter-of-a-century.

Bridgeheads were thrown across the mighty Irrawaddy river, and Mandalay itself invested. Mission after mission created explosion and holocaust as we blasted away with TNT and the venomous mix of twenty-millimetre shells. Though repeatedly hit, the aircraft seemed to share our own fantastic good fortune, and the ragged holes pumped through them were soon patched up. I was still leading "A" Flight's six aircraft, and from time to time led the Squadron on occasions when the heroic efforts of the ground crews enabled us to put up a full dozen planes. Top brass frequently visited us to egg us on, and on one immortal occasion a covey of visiting generals, including Slim, General Officer Commanding the theatre, accompanied by their RAF opposite numbers, dropped in to cheer us on our way just before take-off on the umpteenth trip to Mandalay; the Army had been let down by England and had run out of shells for their big guns, so the Hurribombers had been brought in as a sort of flying artillery. Before climbing into the cockpit for take-off, it was customary to anticipate nature's more elementary demands of the hours to follow, thereby avoiding at least one discomfort. About half-way through, my concentration was disturbed by the roar of the distinguished visitors' approaching jeeps, followed by a hush. But very decently they waited until I'd finished and had adjusted my attire before coming solemnly forward for the introductions and the honeyed, if now slightly hackneyed, phrases of goodwill and encouragement.

Bob Monkland, a Flight Lieutenant, joined us from a photographic reconnaissance unit to fill the gap which I had been plugging as commander of "A" Flight; because he was unfamiliar with our ground attack techniques, especially dive-bombing, he flew as my Number Two until he could familiarise himself with our special skills. To and from Mandalay the Squadron flew several times a day for nearly a week, plastering high explosive into the stubborn Jap positions until we too ran out of bombs. Fortunately by then everybody was utterly exhausted, and the remnants of the enemy soldiery obligingly beat it towards Siam, hotly pursued by the Army. Basically there was no doubt that the Japanese were better jungle soldiers than the British, African or Indian troops who we were supporting. Apart from their fanaticism, based on a religious belief endowed with a quality of delusion, they could travel light and live off the land, a handful of rice and a piece of raw fish being sufficient daily sustenance. They were also able to rely on the support of the Burmese peasants, who found them more akin than they did us. But no amount of courage or independent initiative could alone withstand the sheer weight of metal which was thrown at them from land, sea and air. They fought literally to the death; little wonder they took so much overcoming.

I saw my first live Japanese soldier close up, one of the small handful taken prisoner throughout that bloody campaign. We had just concluded a successful trip, destroying a target given us by radio by an operational RAF pilot spending his "rest" attached to an infantry unit a few yards from the Nips. His flying knowledge, combined with on-the-spot observation, enabled him to feed us information from his Visual Control Post, whereby we could strike instantly. "Hey, Muffin Red One," came the VCP's voice over the radio, "would you like to see a Nip?"

"A live one?" I queried.

"Yes, a real live one. He's just been captured. I'll have him put in the field alongside the pagoda you're just approaching. Don't take his head off with your wing-tip — we want him for interrogation."

Down we went to investigate the strange creature standing between two askaris in a field alongside a bleached pagoda by a dusty road, but disappointingly he seemed to have only two legs and one head.

Jock Ingman's bombs hung up on him and he could not shake them off. Operated by percussion fuses they relied on the density of the air at ground level to detonate them, so one could not land with them still attached beneath the wings without the likelihood of their exploding as the plane descended. There were a number of prescriptions for the situation: to shake the bombs off you could dive then pull up sharply, slow-roll, bunt (the reverse of a loop), but as sometimes happened the bombs stuck on remoreselessly. The only thing for it was to point the plane towards the enemy lines and bale out, but Ingman decided to risk landing. He should not have done so, but there is no way you can compel a pilot to do this or that short of shooting him down. As he levelled off for his landing the bombs exploded. It was a pity that he was not killed outright; the severe injuries he received meant that he lingered on in decreasing health for some time, before dying as a young man.

That sort of sadness was alleviated by the antics of one of our several genuine eccentrics. Van Hooseten, a South African, was that *rara avis*, the frontiersman of a century earlier, with all the exuberance and practical humour of the breed, and a veritable walrus moustache to boot. Lying peacably on one's campbed at night a great hymn would envelop the tented encampment, to the tune of *Jerusalem*, but the words were "Van Hoos-e-ten, Van Hoos-e-ten, Lift up your voice and sing", invariably followed by roars of wrath from the tent of some young pilots whose guy-ropes he had slacked off. He was basically a decent man and never hoiked out their tent-pegs, which would have collapsed the lot on them, so that all they really had to do was slide out from under the suffocating canvas and tighten up the ropes. Mosaic retaliation was regular, but Van Hooseten accepted it stoically, never stirring until morning even though immersed in the fabric of his tent.

We had also acquired a lean, handsome South African Air Force captain, nobody — least of all he — knew how or why he had happened into Central Burma on an RAF squadron. Captain Billy spent many happy hours parodying some of the more ridiculous advertisements in the glossy American magazines which occasionally reached us, such as Jeep-Driver Jones, freshening up with a Seven-up while on manoeuvres in the steamy Arizona jungle. And in stirring "The March of Time" tones he would read out, "Meanwhile, in distant Guadalcanal, Uncle Sam's Marines are locked in hand-to-hand combat with the fanatical Nipponese foe!" "Phooey!" he would continue. "Quite plainly Jeep-Driver Jones was in Arizona at the time, drinking refreshing Seven-up." He was very jungle-happy, the equivalent of the desert "magnoon".

Further comic relief was provided in the form of a Harvard two-seater trainer. There wasn't anything to train about, but the Group Captain also had one, so we constituted a "C" Flight, command of which was entrusted to me. Let it be recorded that never was a Flight more intensively commanded. Every weekend one of the Harvards flew the four hundred miles to Calcutta, empty but for a couple of pilots, and every Monday morning at eight a.m. promptly it was back, under penalty of stern retribution, with the two pilots and as many crates of booze as fitted in to the rear compartment from which the radio and other equipment had been removed. From then on we were thus able to boost our intake of medicine necessary for the white man in those climes. The alcoholic content of the local gin, whisky and brandy was pretty low, but in any event a man's capacity is considerably enlarged in the tropics, where metabolism is accentuated. When my turn came for the Calcutta liquor run, I left the business side of the operation to my co-pilot, and sloped off to my friends of Number 52 Dakota Squadron, stationed at Dumdum, the Calcutta field where we landed — they used to do mail runs, including one along the east coast of the sub-continent and down to Ceylon. We left Dumdum at three-thirty on Saturday morning, flew to Cuttack, Vizagapatam, Madras and thence Colombo, where we arrived in time for tea with the Wrens. Sunday morning saw the Dakota's return, to be back at Dumdum by the evening, and I was back at Sinthe with the replenished Harvard in time for breakfast on Monday morning — after all, what was a three thousand mile trip to spend Saturday night in good company? The second such trip saw a contretemps. As we took off from Madras for Colombo one of the Dakota's engines failed, and we underwent the novel experience of flying below tree height, until the plane succumbed and span into the ground from fifty feet up, pirouetted gently on one wing-tip, then slewed violently round before coming to a halt on the brink of a steep ravine; the operation broke the plane's back, then it promptly burst into flames. Had it slid a further five feet we would have plunged down among the rocks and would certainly have been killed. But the magical charm was still working away merrily. There followed the mortifying experience of watching the blue flames leap up from my four bottles of gin for Saturday night's party ablaze in the parachute-bag in which I carried them, and I had to be forcibly restrained from rushing to the rescue just as the petrol tanks in the wings exploded. My logbook also perished in the blaze, and it took some time to recover from the combined loss.

Real tragedy struck when the Squadron doctor went out hunting with Bob Monkland, and just off the airstrip, by an adjoining village, they bumped into a Japanese patrol who promptly opened fire, killing the Doc. He was Monkland's only intimate, they being of an age — ancients of twenty-eight or so. The Doc was greatly liked and, armed with whatever weapons could be mustered, to a man the Squadron went off in search of the enemy soldiers, determined to avenge the murder, but by then their quarry must have been miles away. The villagers were pro-Jap, and regularly lit fires by the airstrip as markers for the enemy night-bombers which dropped anti-personnel bombs, from time to time killing and maiming numbers of our men, and sometimes destroying our aircraft. Exploding just above ground level, like our percussion bombs, the a-p bombs shot out blast and shrapnel horizontally. As soon as we heard the distinctive engine note of the bombers we dived into the slit trenches dug beside our tents. They never came by moonlight, and except by moonlight we could not night-fly and oppose them. Except on one occasion when we were tipped off that there was to be an enemy bombing raid, and by virtue of my accumulated six hundred hours of flying Hurricanes I could claim to be the Squadron's most experienced pilot and therefore entitled to tackle the attacker. In a small tent at the end of the strip, my plane alongside, I waited all night for the raiders, who did not come, and I grew colder, more tired and more frightened as night slid towards dawn; by then my knees were knocking so hard I doubt whether I could have taken off anyway. The small hours have seldom encouraged heroism.

Monkland was a strange man, of mercurial temperament, with hooded eyes and a mouth at the same time sensuous and sadistic. He was long and snakelike, and I would imagine utterly fascinating to women. In the Mess, which at the time consisted of only seven of us, he could be the soul of morbidity or the quintessence of vivacity. He had mastered the necesary art of privacy whilst living communally, a kind of spiritual withdrawal which comes easily to the fighter-pilot by virtue of the solitariness of his occupation. Unlike most of us, he had enjoyed a short prewar adult existence, as a journalist living in Paris. He sang in French, Greek and Italian, accompanying himself on a battered old guitar that he managed to hawk around with him. When the atrocious dehydrated food on which we lived was about to be served up by the Indian servant who looked after us, he would enquire: "What delectable morsel have we tonight to tempt the jaded palate, Raymond?" Then, "Bring on the swill!" I too found him fascinating, veering between attraction towards his comparative sophistication and contempt for his fear of bombs, for if he could slide out of a bombing trip he would. He relied on me to cover for him. "Will you take this one today?" he would invariably ask, but casually, when we were called for briefing for a bombing raid. So I continued to lead "A" Flight, although he was its Commander. He wasn't of the stuff of which pilots are made, least of all should he have accepted a posting to a ground attack squadron. I suppose he was the braver for seeing it through, had he been able to do so. He was not to survive much longer,

198

already marked out as the victim of another tragedy, of which the Doc's death was a part.

We bought cockerels from the villagers to supplement our inadequate diet. They crowed in Burmese, a strange noise — "Ur-a-ur-ur" which presumably meant "Cock-a-doodle-doo". They were small and insipid and thoroughly deserved to be hypnotised which we did by holding them head down to a strip of white paper. They would stay in that position for hours, while we tried to teach them to crow in English, but they never learnt. When not hypnotised they crowed day and night, and with the grasshoppers and crickets kept up a perpetual racket of noise. Scraggy cattle mooned aimlesssly among our tents, now and again stopping to wrap a lazy tongue round some withered blade of grass which they had difficulty in eradicating. If successful they were so worn out by the effort that they tended to collapse on the spot, usually across the guy ropes, whence no amount of abuse or hurled sods could dislodge them until they had rested, when after emitting surplus liquids from various cavities they teetered away on unsure hooves. Ants of every kind abounded, and one ate and drank them, knowing it but not caring. Dung-beetles, known as heavy bombers, whirred blindly round the inside of the tents, a cumbersome and easy target for our irritation. Locusts dropped into one's drink, furry caterpillars lodged in one's boots, lizards dozing in one's steel trunk scuttled for safety betwixt neck and shirt collar, jettisoning their tails in their anxiety for escape. Rats foraged round the tents, their impressive digestive powers enabling them to consume soap and even the standard Service biscuit rations known as "hard tack", before we retaliated with our .38s. We found a chameleon and made a home for it on a rope strung between the tent poles, where it caught flies with a long thin and extraordinarily agile tongue. We were disappointed in its vaunted colour changes which ranged from muddy grey to muddy brown, with the emphasis on mud.

Back to operating strength, we undertook Squadron formation take-offs and landings of twelve aircraft. It was no different from taking off or landing as a pair. All that was required was to formate on the leader of one's section, who formated on the section ahead of him, and so on; on take-off the formation leader allowed for the fact that there was a slight interval between opening his throttle and the next man following suit, and that by the time the twelfth man had done so there was a not inconsiderable time gap. So his throttle movements were slow rather than rapid, smooth rather than sudden. He held his aircraft down after it had attained flying speed, so that when he lifted off the last man also had flying speed and could lift off too. That was something not allowed for in Number 33 Squadron's formation aerobatics. Similarly, on landing the leader touched down rather faster than when flying independently, and further up the strip, again to allow for the time lag in throttle adjustment at the rear of the formation, and to provide ample runway room for all twelve aircraft. And he had to keep his throttle fairly wide open after touchdown, only applying brake after the last man had radioed "Green Two pancaked." Of course, that kind of exercise was only possible because the Jap fighter opposition had evanesced, and there was no risk of the formation being "jumped" with its trousers down.

Bombs dropped with delayed fuses anticipated a further bridgehead thrown across the broad Irrawaddy at Nyaungu as the Fourteenth Army rolled inexorably towards Rangoon, and we carried out dawn patrols armed with our bombs and cannon, waiting the VCP's call to specific targets. A squadron of United States Army Air Force Mitchell bombers arrived to join in the fun, bringing with them their own Flying Control Officer, Marty Mallenkow, who took over completely. He was one of life's natural hosts, always on the give, and we revelled in his flow of wisecracks. When you asked permission to take off you'd be told you could try if you liked; when you wanted to land he would ask you to stand by while he held the runway steady. But as we taxied in we used to ask him to confirm that we had landed, so softly and beautifully had we accomplished the manoeuvre. The Mitchell crews were a hoot, going off on bombing trips wearing ridiculous green jockey-caps and with long cigars poking out of their mouths. They battered a Jap stronghold called Okkshitpin and radioed back, "Mission successful, target renamed OKKPIN!" We used to follow them on to an already pulverised target, between us blasting resistance into the dust. A squadron of USAAF Thunderbolt divebombers navigated less well than the multi-crewed Mitchells, and wherever we saw them knocking hell out of the ground we knew that was not the target; thereby they assisted our own navigation, albeit negatively. The Americans were distinctive, not only because of their jockey-caps and cigars but because they were emblazoned with bold badges declaring their allegiance to the US Twentieth Army Air Force, their breasts bedecked with rows of gay medal ribbons which in our more meretricious moments we rather envied. Although only those disporting them knew what they were for — we suspected that such a plethora must represent such activities as a week at sea, first-class cooking in the field, punctuality at work, neat penmanship, or even outstanding bravery in action — they represented a sound psychology as well as being terribly colourful. There wasn't a man who didn't have four or five rows of them, perhaps twenty to thirty medals, and Generals and suchlike were swathed from shoulder to waist and then overflowed on to the opposite side. I suppose the initiated could read them, like some kind of adventure story. Some of the Americans painted on their Mitchells "The Great SNAFU Fleet". We found out that "SNAFU" was an acronym for "Situation Normal — All Fouled Up".

Supplies arriving by air were frequently dropped at the end of a parachute, whose silk was converted into scarves, handkerchiefs and so on. Out of two or three 'chutes I constructed small tents and erected them around the outdoor wooden thrones which served as WCs, thereby providing a degree of unaccustomed privacy. They had a kind of flapdoor, operated from the throne by a strange system of ropes. This must undoubtedly have been my major war contribution. When we were visited by an ENSA party of two or three men and an equal number of women, the one and only such experience I was to encounter between 1940 and 1946, we held a party in their honour in the Officers' Mess, and invited the pilots of the other squadrons in the neighbourhood. Another guest was a Buddha, which somebody had stupidly taken from a pagoda, but which was returned a day later rather than have dark sinister strangers following us to the ends of the globe for ever more. The competition for the ENSA girls was blazing hot, and after repulsing a mild approach from the comedian of the party, a middle-aged queer who later became well known and who must therefore remain nameless, I retired early from the fray, to commune briefly with nature beneath one of the parachute-tents. My solitary splendour was suddenly interrupted by the sound of approaching voices, recognisable as belonging to Eastman and one of the ENSA girls. Hastily I yanked the rope which shut the flapdoor, and the voices receded in the direction of the jungle behind me. But there they seemed to pause and linger, dropping to passionate murmuring, and my embarrassment at the sounds which then ensued confined me to frozen immobility in the tiny tent for a further ten minutes, during which I almost fainted for lack of air. Thank heavens they finished at last, the murmuring resumed, and they made their way past my silken prison, so that at last, in a state bordering collapse, I could at last pull the appropriate rope and stagger out into the night air and to my campbed. I had been much too decent about the incident, and realised I should just have marched in on the pair of them with a jolly greeting. I got my own back on Eastman next morning, and indeed sporadically throughout the years that followed.

Monkland was becoming increasingly depressed. Turning to me as a confidant, he disclosed a desperately unhappy love affair with a married woman in Calcutta, whose husband was serving elsewhere in the Services. It transpired that Monkland too was married, each of them had a child or children, and the situation was hopeless. There was no comfort I could offer — I didn't have the experience. It was against that background, combined with the death of his friend the Doctor, and his own fear of the bombs which we carried, that the stage was set for an inevitable tragedy. The magic voice had ceased to whisper in his ear.

In those compressed days, when lifetimes were lived in weeks, and each day was cut out to be one's likely last, the time was not long arriving when Monkland was airborne with a pair of percussion-detonated bombs beneath the wings of his Hurricane, and they hung up on him. He called up on the radio for the decks to be cleared so that he could come in to land. Obdurately he refused the advice given him over the radio to try and shake the bombs clear or, failing that, to climb to five thousand feet, point the Hurricane towards the jungle, and bale out. After poor Ingman's disaster we all knew what was likely to happen if he tried to land. "I'm coming in," he insisted, and nothing could dissuade him. It was as if he knew he would die by the agency of the things he most feared and, more than that, as if he wanted to die. No sooner had the Hurricane levelled off on its approach than the bombs exploded, hurling the wreckage of the plane onto its back, as it slithered upside down along the dirt runway in a searing sheet of flame. Monkland died instantly. Thus were his conflicts resolved.

Close to the third anniversary of my exile thoughts of home became obsessive; night after night I fell into uneasy sleep with my brain whirring to the accompaniment of *When Johnny Comes Marching Home*, the music of the nights comforting the buffeted mind, and in my dreams I was back home and happy so that I woke up laughing out loud with the sheer pleasure of it, knowing that the rosy tomorrow had arrived, I was home, and it was all over at last, the long weary exile, the strain which we never consciously acknowledged. The slow flapping of the drab canvas walls in the early morning light shattered the dream, realisation slowly dawned that I was still in Burma, and bitter disappointment had to be gulped down in one quick draught and another day faced, while the scaly skin of imperturbability hid all desire and emotion. When disappointment is no longer unexpected, almost accepted, one has begun to grow up. Even the trite consideration that every day was one day nearer the end saw its consolation dissolve, as doubt increasingly queried — nearer the end of what? of exile? life? youth? a familiar existence? A war which had occupied our total adulthood? But dreams were not only of returning home but also of more mundane matters such as the stomach. God! I thought, next time I get to Calcutta I'll have a giant steak with fried onions and all the trimmings and a couple of large fried eggs on top of the lot. I did, but a stomach shrunken to the size needed to cope with a campaign diet could not accept more than a couple of mouthfuls of the succulent fare.

The Black Prince had been replaced by Harry Cutler, son of a Grimsby Norwegian. "Grimmy Danes" as they are known, are plentiful, but Harry was a rarer specimen. Already sporting the Distinguished Flying Cross, his leadership of Number 11 Squadron in the time of its supreme warlike glory gained him a coveted Distinguished Service Order, in his own generous words an award to the Squadron rather than to a man. A former racing driver, he taught me how to skid and unskid a jeep on the slushy jungle tracks; he could really make a jeep do anything except sit up and talk. He smoked a hundred cigarettes a day, from the first slowly-reached one as dawn penetrated the charred remains of successive mosquito nets to the last one which habitually set them on fire. We lost count of the number of times we had to run over to his tent to extinguish him, for when Harry fell asleep he was absolutely out. Rumour had it that when he went to Calcutta on one of the Harvard trips he slept right through the weekend. He was a highly skilled pilot. He and I had a very private arrangement which enabled us to slope off on our own while the rest were still sleeping. "Up at sparrow's fart tomorrow?" he invited. As the first glimmer of dawn showed, "Okay," Harry quietly woke me, "let's go and strike a blow for democracy. Clears the old head a bit," he added as he released morning wind — "better an empty house than a bad tenant!" I enjoyed flying as his Number Two on those dawn cab-ranks, when one patrolled the battle area, armed with bombs and cannon, waiting for the VCP to announce a target, usually a bunker position where the Japs had entrenched and could not be winkled out by the infantry. Back for breakfast we talked music. He was a Beethoven and Brahms expert.

The Squadron blasted oil and arms dumps and other military installations near Pagan, a great city of pagodas, leaving raging infernos where we struck. That assault had to be carefully timed so that we arrived on target at last light. That meant that we made a night return and landing. With green lights on our starboard wingtips, red on our port, and white lights at our tails, we huddled into the usual tight formation as we approached the strip, peeling off one after the other as we did in daylight. When we had landed safely one of the hard-bitten Chiefies was in tears; in his wrinkled eyes we were just a gang of boys. Charmed young men whose lives the charm had not yet deserted. By now, most of the pilots who had been at Tamu had been replaced by a bunch of cheerful enthusiastic youngsters. As one of the old-timers I was sent to India on a short course to learn the latest missiles, including rockets, which I found extraordinarily well-behaved. Provided range and aircraft speed were gauged accurately it was virtually impossible not to hit the target. Although all of us on the course were very experienced pilots we still had to defer to our instructors, largely heavily-decorated survivors of the Battle of Britain days. Poker had been eliminated from my life that wet Saturday in the drying-room at Tern Hill, and here bridge followed, for Squadron Leader Blunt, who had not one but two DSOs and not one but two DFCs formed an ad hoc organisation called IABSSEA (Imperial Anti-Bridge Society, South East Asia). The founder, and indeed its sole member, he spent his evenings wandering among the innocuous tables giving stentorian advice. His justification for his Organisation was that bridge interfered with more serious convivial pleasures, and he was probably right. Anyway, he broke my spirit.

While on the course, Tom Sutherland flew into the ground and was killed instantly — at twenty-six the voice no longer whispered in his ear. His remains were scraped together and coffined in a hastily-constructed box. We gave him a formal burial, complete with firing party. It was a burning day as six of us bore him on our bony shoulders, the box leaking his remains over my neck and voracious flies swarming over me, feasting, as the heavy deadweight bit into my scant flesh. Standing beside the open grave while the padre gabbled his absurd words, the rising stench was all that was real. I resented the ridiculous litany; it was almost obscene. I swayed while the flies tormented me, my neck was sticky, and only an enormous effort kept me from toppling forward into the grave. The rifle-shots rang out, and we saluted.

A day later I left the Mess to cross the few yards to my hut to change for the evening meal and fell flat on my face. I crawled the short distance on hands and knees, and spent the next ten days overcoming the jaundice which had struck me, a stinking and dangerous disease prevalent in the tropics, whose odour permeates everything and which earmarks its victims for cirrhosis of the liver sooner or later. After the first few days I was strong enough to get to the shower, disgusted at the smell of my own body, which no amount of washing seemed able to refresh.

As soon as I was back on my feet I returned to Burma, where XI Squadron was operating in the vicinity of Alanmyo. At the VCP's behest I pooped clouds of shells into a dried-up wadi, although there was nothing to be seen but scrubby vegetation and kicked-up dust. But by the time I was back at base a signal had been received that upwards of thirty Japanese sodiers had been killed in the attack — they had been laying land-mines, which I had exploded. The Army sent me a treasured trophy, a Japanese flag, rare and coveted. Every enemy soldier receives one before going off to the wars, inscribed with good luck messages. They wore them round their midriffs, believing that they were thereby preserved from harm. Mine was holed and stained with blood. For another poor bastard the charm had failed.

We battered the area for several days, shooting up tanks, troops and gun positions. Many of the Hurricanes were hit. With our long-range fuel tanks we were a lumbering target, capable of only a hundred and thirty-five miles an hour. At Yenanyaung, hard on the heels of the USAAF Mitchells, the Hurricanes dived through a thick curtain of enemy flak to bomb the oilfields, leaving dense columns of smoke hundreds of feet high, and shattered rigs splayed crazily among the flames. Hume, killed as he dived, went into the ground with his plane and bombs. A shell through Dace's cockpit sent him home wounded and bleeding, but his charm survived. I looked out at jagged shell-holes patterning my wings, wondering why the petrol tanks inside them had not exploded, and shrugged metaphorically and physically. We were past caring. We were jungle-happy. Fear, like pleasure, reposes largely in the imagination, and is therefore anticipatory or retrospective. Both emotions often elude full appreciation at the moment they are experienced. As tradition demanded, we gathered together Hume's few private baubles — wallet, letters, photographs and logbook — and sent them with a round-robin to his widowed mother, but there was an impersonality about it. Heaven knows whether she ever received them.

Despite the herculean efforts of the ground crews we now had only three serviceable aircraft. Courtesy of the gremlins, cannibalisation helped to remedy the deficiency slightly. Pilkington went down in flames, leaning forward unconscious as his plane miraculously landed itself in a paddyfield by a jungle track along which an Army convoy happened to be moving. We orbited as they raced to pull him clear of the burning wreck, to save his charmed life. He was badly burnt. Maclay went mad, wandering in the jungle naked and bleeding, his eyes unseeing, holding aloft the small silver cross he wore round his thin neck, and mumbling

210

unintelligibly. He had withdrawn from reality. Van Hooseten disappeared; we found him lying unclothed in a thorn bush, his body lacerated and streaked with his own blood, his hair anointed with molten chocolate. Curious, we wondered where he had got it from, and turned resolutely from both incidents. "Good for you, good for me, good for all the soldiers," Captain Bill announced.

Again we packed camp, the Dakotas arrived, and we moved to Magwe, in the forlorn desolate area of central Burma immediately east of the Irrawaddy, south of its conflux with the Chindwin — a parched dusty land covered with desert scrub and a few scraggy palms. With bombs and cannon we ranged east to the Siamese border and south towards Rangoon where a new Army was put ashore and was forcing its way to join up with the Forgotten Fourteenth. The Burma campaign was approaching its end. Here and there pockets of fanatical Japs held out, but the rout was almost complete. Wherever they assembled we blew them apart, destroying their oil and ammunition dumps, and divebombing their temporary headquarters with what was now a fantastic accuracy. The villages harbouring their remnants were set ablaze; the Squadron was inspired beyond denial, and the daylong strikes, one after the other, could not fail. Each target we were given was hit and destroyed, as we wove a pattern of indelible fire throughout the land. But although the delivery of death had become our special skill, and as young men we were by our nature accustomed to respond to the stirring call to arms against an enemy believed evil, not far beneath the surface dwelt an intense youthful desire to do good, to benefit our fellow men — at times a suffocating thing — and to that extent a crusader spirit was nurtured. A feeling of worthwhileness in the destruction of what we considered evil was part of our camaraderie, with our community of hardship, disdain for the uninitiated, anxiety for battle, and especially what might be called the mystique of elitism.

One afternoon by the Irrawaddy I beheld the remains of a decapitated man floating slowly downstream in a cocoon of his own slime. Where his head had once joined his neck a string of skin tendrils swayed gently on the surface of the water. From his bloated belly shiny white maggots bred from his entrails as he sailed slowly past, the ugly vision seeming to mock at my live warmth and wholeness. I knew then that death is of the body alone. It dies and quickly rots into foulness. Burn, inter, sink the mere shell. That which is called "soul" never dies. I knew then that after the crushing of my flesh I would live on, wherever something of me had brushed off on to others — a smile, a scowl, a kindness, a detriment, my intonations, habits, expressions, failings, influences — good or ill — all these I knew would remain in those still tied to their bodies, and would in turn partially brush off on to other living souls. I knew I could never die; death of the body held no fear, for my soul would live in the memories which the living retained of me, sweetness and kindness or hatred and abhorrence, depending on the impact made during my bodily life. And the infinitesimal part of my personality which had brushed off on to others, like theirs on to me, had already become a permanent part of the recipient, and thus we were all immortal. Whether our souls are in heaven or hell depended on how we had impacted on others. Notwithstanding the carnage I was helping to wreak, I felt suddenly at peace. I saw nothing fearsome in death, which was as much part of life as my conduct and thoughts, the conclusion at any moment of a natural and inevitable cycle. Woman gives birth astride the grave. Remove the dimension of time and we are dead as soon as conceived; curtail it, and the diminished circle is nevertheless a perfect form. Death was no sadder than the life of which it formed part; though it seemed sad to die regretting what one had done, or worse what one had not. Yet I knew also that I needed a moment of peace before death, and that I would probably die fighting death, unable to achieve that essential pause. It will all be over quickly, we used to joke, Just a big bang, then curtains! That was not what I wanted but that's how it would be — a mighty, final, ultra-blasphemous oath, the ultimate and therefore the mightiest, then the big bang, swift pain and oblivion. I shrugged it off.

We were told of the German surrender. On VE-Day we were expected to celebrate, but to us Germany, Europe, Blighty, were of a different world a lifetime distant. Our war was continuing, and the Japanese were still in Thailand and Malaya. Our mood evoked an order to celebrate, and sulkily the airmen gathered round an absurd official bonfire before sloping off to their tents at the earliest opportunity. Next morning we were out bombing and strafing as usual, though the end was nearer than we realised.

At Taungdaw, a Ghurka company, cut off for three days, broke out after our repeated strikes, in the course of which one of them won the Victoria Cross. Nearby we paved the way for a successful infantry attack up a long muddy hill on top of which the Japanese had entrenched, defying a weeklong assault by the Army. As the Hurribombers dived to attack, the infantry churned bravely but sluggishly through glutinous mud more than ankle deep. They waved, the position was taken, and we were rewarded with another coveted trophy — a Japanese officer's sword. Deserted by his charm, Big Pilkie crashed and died. Chiefy Barnard, one of the senior engineers, had endured too much and fired his .38 to blast out his own brains. On our next mission we were ordered to bomb one wing, some twenty feet long, of an L-shaped building at Kwema, which housed the last enemy general in Burma and his staff officers. With uncanny precision six Hurricanes dropped their bombs slap on to the tiny target, obliterating it, such was our dive-bombing accuracy. Silently, the familiar jagged holes appeared in the upper surface of my starboard wing where a Japanese shell had crashed into the main spar which held it to the fuselage. The Hurricane rocked under the impact, and by all normal standards the wing should have broken away, to plunge me to my death; miraculously my luck continued to hold, as I nursed the quivering plane back to base. We returned to two signals. The first was from Air Headquarters, South East Asia: "11 Squadron cease to operate with effect from 16/5/45"; the other from Advanced Headquarters, Fourteenth Army, read: "A sad farewell to our old friends."

The farewell to perfection, albeit of destruction, was indeed sad, but it had been a banging end, ablaze with glory. And who knew what adventure lay ahead for those of us still left.

CHAPTER
ELEVEN

Zipper

Shrouded in the exciting mystery of ignorance we pulled out from Burma to re-equip for the invasion of Malaya. We flew the remaining obsolete Hurricanes first to Calcutta, then by stages down to Chettinad, deep in the south of India, where a splendid unused airfield located, in accordance with RAF tradition, in the middle of nowhere, extended a restrained welcome of orderly virgin bamboo huts. The supporting two hundred-odd ground crew were to follow several weeks later, after a patchy journey by train and truck. As one of the Squadron songs had it, "They're moving Legs Eleven once again." Hardly had we settled in than word arrived that unfortunately we'd been sent to the wrong airfield, so off we flew to the right one, equally desolate and virgin, called Tanjore. There a new message awaited which was to launch eight of our small number to the regional capital, Bangalore, to collect new trucks for the Squadron's use. Bangalore was the headquarters town of Southern Army Command, India, another cosy headquarters billets stuffed with starched headquarters wallahs, so that we were put in mind of the famous song about ACSEA, Air Command, South East Asia, those brave warriors roughing it in the wilds of Kandy, in central Ceylon, surrounded by young Women's Royal Naval Service ladies:

Why be miserable, why be miserable,
ACSEA isn't yet at war,
Sitting down at Kandy, feeling fine and dandy,
Thinking operations are a bore;
Why worry about the enemy,
We've always got the Wrennery,
The Queen's is never short of liquor;
So just soft-pedal and you'll get another medal
And the war won't be over any quicker.

Sitting on your bum, twiddling your thumb,
Don't get covered in remorse,
Just say when you want the latest gen
And you'll shove off to Blighty on a course;

So shout Hurray, the war's okay,
We're having lots of fun,
Six-hour day and bags of pay
And f— all ever done,

So, why be miserable, why be miserable,
You may never see a Zero,
Sitting down at ACSEA with your finger up your
jacksie —
You'll be another South East Asia hero!

It was perhaps a little bitter, but notwithstanding our rough jungle attire our feeling towards the creamy ones was disdainful, and we would not have swapped places with them for anything in the world. At Kandy the Supremo held court among seven thousand "courtiers" including the pretty ladies, all of them in service uniforms adorned with the same campaign medal ribbons as had been issued to us.

At the Bangalore Club we were directed to tents in the courtyard, rather than the elegant chambers within the cool of the full-up marble palace (no room at the inn, we thought); in the course of a slightly prolonged stay, due to nobody at the lorry depot having heard about vehicles for Number 11 Squadron, we made ourselves at home. After all, we were used to tents.

Our first entry into the austerely grand Club came straight out of a Wild West film. As we removed our stained and jungly slough hats and hung them on the hatstand in the noble entrance hall, all eyes were on us. "Perhaps we ought to hang up our guns as well," I hissed. We were wearing gunbelts, complete with armoury of revolver, ammunition pouch, commando dagger and kukri. Slightly sheepishly, in the gaze of the incredulous pongos, we unbuckled the broad belts and hung the weapons alongside our hats. We were conscious of the inelegance of our battle gear — crumpled faded shirts and slacks, puttees and marching boots — in contrast with the sleek, shiny green jackets, knife-edged trousers and fancy shoes of the Club's regulars. Self-consciously we made a passage to the dining-room, where magnificent food was served by a veritable army of waiters in sparkling white, wearing coat-length tunics, turbans, and elegant bandannas. Punka-wallahs tugged tirelessly at the ropes and pulleys attached at one end to their big toes and at the other to outsize fans suspended from the lofty ceilings. At a dance the same night in the romantically chandeliered ballroom we really came into our own, though thereby we incurred the animosity of enjealoused — nay, enraged — Army gentlemen, presumably husbands, fiancés or lovers. For we were lean and brown and hungry-looking, operational fighter-pilots straight out of the Burmese jungle, fit and muscular.

Oh Lush Thrush! where are you now? Was I for you justified in undergoing the indignity of seriously attempted onslaught by that outraged, baying platoon of pongos chasing me through wild streams, over harsh rockeries and spiky flowerbeds, among thorny trees and shrubs, bent on destroying their panting, flushed yet still innocent quarry in the very gardens of the illustrious Bangalore Club? And yet, as the days went by and they grew to know us better, did they not also grow to like and accept us, rough edges and all, and realise that we too had our Boy Scouts' honour? At least, Brown Jobs, you did not begrudge Harry Pate his faded lady whom you had all in turns enjoyed through your hard war years and, warriors that you were at heart, you conceded him his unimportant triumph. Harry was the only one to return victorious and full of his virility to the courtyard encampment and the flagons of gin which the bearers spent their time buying for us. Would you believe, staunch soldiers, that we

219

were knocking back a bottle-and-a-half each daily, and you must admit that never once did you see any one of us more than the slightest bit tiddly. Yes, our lean brown frames absorbed the alcohol effortlessly. Then when at last our trucks were ready you did not want to let us go; not you, pongos, still less your fair ladies. But we were made of sterner stuff, tempered by war and violent death, and we were off, slouch hats, gunbelts, gin-thirsts and all, off to prepare for the next round of our unending war, off on our continuous exile, and the tents in the courtyard were barren once again.

The road back wound along red-brown tracks rutted with the ox-wagon wheels of centuries, and was lined with green shade and fragrant bougainvillea flowers peeping brilliantly over mud walls to ensnare us, through villages perfumed by accumulated mountains of dried and drying dung whose prickling odour hung like a heavy, permeating cloud. We wove through a vast red plain bearing hundreds of thousands of white-clad peasants in fertile fields, backs baked by the blatant sun as they bent plying ancient implements to scratch at the dusty red hide of their yielding earth. Then with a sudden shriek and a rush, a naked brown devil leapt out of nowhere, startling us, like a whirlwind of dust painted red and blue and yellow, slap in front of the leading truck, leaping high into the air and screeching and shaking dementedly. The convoy braked to a dirt-flinging halt, and the devil could be seen to be grinning, filed teeth flashing among alternating dark gaps, long black snakes of oiled hair glistened down to his sweat-streaked, vibrating body, his skinny nakedness covered only with an abbreviated leather loincloth the same hue as his almost black skin. In his right hand he carried a great whip which he raised and pointed at us significantly, in a dramatic pose.

By now we were surrounded by a band of equally naked savages carrying long spears. We did not know what to make of the situation. So far there was no indication of aggression and it seemed unnecessary to draw our guns, which were clearly visible. Slowly the devil moved into a gyrating dance, increasing steadily in abandonment, then suddenly he extended his arm to crack the great whip resoundingly behind his thin back, screeching; then danced again, then screeched and cracked, for a full ten minutes while the scraggy warriors stood round us grinning enthusiastically and stinking under the hot sun, and all the while one of them beat a drum, and one played a reedy pipe-tune. The music stopped and the dance stopped, the devil put his hand behind his back then brought it in front of him, to show us that it was dripping with blood. In a single bound he leapt into the air and jumped around to reveal his back. It was lacerated beyond belief, pouring blood over yards of horizontal blue weals and scars, presumably from past performances. Suspicious that the entertainment carried pre-sacrificial overtones we did not know whether to applaud or fire warning shots. Nor could we just move on, as we were hemmed in by the scrawny brown spearmen. The devil continued to bound, shrieking shrilly, then a cheer-leader among the warriors mumbled at us encouragingly,

221

the light dawned, we realised that the filed teeth were not to eat us with, and relieved we threw handfuls of rupee coins into the dust. That worked the oracle, and after what we took to be expressions of demoniac appreciation, the star and the warriors moved to one side to let us pass, waving and leaping, and yelling wild farewells as we ground off down the dusty track. Later we learnt that we had probably run into a section of a wedding party and that the whole gang of them, drunk as lords on local alcohol, had simply been feeling friendly and a bit exhibitionist, like any bloke in a pub. The devil would be a second-degree fakir, not particularly spiritual but trained to withstand pain.

A further signal had been received at Tanjore, confiding that Chettinad had after all been our correct destination and to make our way there as soon as we could. When we arrived, the rest of the Squadron was already cosily ensconced in the best of the bamboo billets. Our new planes arrived, the very latest fashion from Blighty, the newest Spitfires. From the 135 miles an hour of the clapped-out old Hurricanes we escalated to a cool 350 in the Spit XIV, or 450 if really in a hurry, though at that speed you might lose a wing, as one pilot did; he was below earth in a sizable crater before he had a chance to bale out. To start the mighty Griffon 65 engine required the use of an explosive charge — there were five largish cartridges and thus you had five chances, by then if you hadn't caught the engine with your throttle you were stuck. The engine's power caused severe take-off problems as the fuselage tended to try and turn around the gigantic five-bladed airscrew, rather than the other way round — an exaggerated version of engine torque. The result was that on all except the most gentle of take-offs the Spitfire would attempt a violent swing to starboard, often successfully. Indeed, one of our pilots never succeeded in mastering the take-off technique, invariably taking off along a right-angled track. In due course he hacked out his own runway, shaped like a boomerang, and many were the scars and skid marks along that unique configuration. Our anxiety increased at the intelligence that we were down there prefatory to embarking on — of all things — an aircraft-carrier, which would take us to the coast of Malaya which was to be invaded. Once aboard, the only way off the carrier being by means of a deck take-off, we studied hard at the necessary techniques, which involved the sudden application of maximum power and thus the creation of maximum torque. What we had to do was rev the engine up steadily against the holding power of the brakes, then as the plane started to slide against the brakes release them, at the same moment pushing the throttle wide open, applying full left rudder and full left aileron. The airscrew of practically every plane ever designed turned to the right, so that any swing was to the left — away from the side of an aircraft-carrier where the bridge, funnels and so on are located. The Spit XIV's airscrew turned to the left, so that the familiar swing to starboard meant that the plane would crash into the carrier's superstructure. The clever fellows who had dreamed up the idea of a deck take-off

223

for the RAF must have searched long and hard to find a plane with an airscrew which rotated the wrong way.

A fresh batch of new pilots, joining their first squadron and culled from training schools, outnumbered the old hands, and the handful of Burma men tended to herd into a clique. Our eight weeks of intensive training were interspersed with outings to an improbable restaurant we found in the middle of nowhere, where there was an accumulation of pre-war Scotch whisky. Pondicherry was not too distant, and boasted a gin refinery whence we imported splendid French eight-gallon flagons of the stuff. On the camp our spare hours were enlivened by music played on our ancient gramophone alongside a mysterious artificial pool filled with bloated bullfrogs. We were forbidden to swim in it, nobody knew why. But along its sides at night a group of pilots sat idly chatting, swilling copious quantities of Pondicherry gin and singing nostalgically *The Moonlight's There Tonight Along the Chindwin*. I contrived a couple of weekends in Colombo, flying one of the Hurricanes still awaiting the knacker's yard, haring along at eight thousand feet over the archipelago which almost joins the toe of India with Ceylon.

Transferring to Madura, another of the unused chain of airfields built in southern India against a Japanese invasion, we joined up with 17 Squadron into a new fighter-reconnaissance Wing; 17 had also operated in Burma. An Army instructor taught us how to "range", so that we could direct artillery fire on to an enemy position; cameras were fixed in the side and belly of the Spitfires and we learnt how to operate them. The

Spitfires were now Mark XVIII's. An artificial aircraft-carrier deck marked out on the concrete runway enabled us to practise getting airborne without plunging into the hypothetical hoggin. By now familiar with the powerful Spit and the take-off technique, the old sweats among us itched to get on with the invasion, to experience anew the excitement and satisfaction of operational flying. In my fourth year of exile I knew I would never again see England; disembarrassed of home and family they had passed out of my thoughts. Spiritually, I believed I had achieved a catharsis, which like the ACSEA phoenix symbol, directed towards a single-minded purpose untrammelled by other considerations. The airfield was near the town of Madura where we glimpsed intimate details of Indian provincial life, wandering around bazaars and temples, sitting in rooms of refreshment, and gawking at the monstrous juggernaut tower parked in the town square, beneath whose enormous wooden wheels scores of men annually sacrificed themselves to the ogre-god — or so it was reported.

Wilburton, one of the new boys already nicknamed "the Desperado", was unconscious for forty-eight hours after having drunk Pondicherry gin non-stop for three solid days, during which he had kept himself awake by liberal doses of benzadrine filched from his survival kit. His was an extreme but by no means isolated case of temporary alcoholism, for by now we had learnt that our "aircraft-carrier" was nothing more than one of the converted "Liberty" ships known as escort-carriers, with a deck length of only 430 feet, a good deal less than one-half that of the standard Fleet carrier, and our eagerness for the take-off required the support of a little Dutch courage. Waiting for the event began to constitute a strain, and I alternated between the familiar conflicts of apprehension and a desire to get on with the job and be operational again, a strain which increased daily as we were briefed for our role in the invasion, code-named "Zipper", and on escape tactics related to the Malay terrain. For the first time we were advised that if captured we should tell the Japanese anything they wanted to know rather than undergo torture. But they were still decapitating captured airmen, an ignominious end not always easy to occlude from the mind. Zipper was calculated to be one of the last battles, one of the final nails in the Japanese coffin, for at last Russia was indulging in a token war in eastern Asia, with an eye to matters territorial, and the Americans were launching mighty air attacks by day and night against the Japanese homeland. News came, first of the atomic bombing of Hiroshima and Nagasaki, followed closely by Japan's unconditional surrender. That night there were gloomy faces in the bamboo Mess; there was no celebration at the ending of the long war, for we knew with a shock that we would soon be pitched into civilian life. What were we to do? What would become of us? Our lives consisted of flying and killing, we knew nothing else, had known nothing else since our schooldays.

That evening a mood of despair speedily set in, and nobody was interested in revelry. Retiring dismally to our bashas, filled with apprehension at the auguries, the deck take-off still ahead began to seem a pointless hazard; surely it would now be cancelled. A few minutes later a red glow lit the night sky as one of the pilots despondently pooped off a Very cartridge, followed by another, then another. The last, borne by a stiff breeze, lodged in the thatched roof of a basha in the front row opposite the Mess, setting it alight. Knowing the high combustibility of the dry bamboo we hastened to fetch water to extinguish the blaze, but within a minute the bungalow was blazing and already its neighbours were ignited. The whole camp was alerted to the serious situation, but the heat and the increasing wind were too much, and to our disbelief and dismay one by one the bashas caught fire, until within thirty minutes the entire camp was burnt to the ground. Mournful and blackened we sat outside the perimeter of smouldering bamboo, beside the few items of personal gear we had managed to salvage. We were lucky to lose only our belongings. Thus, with what became known as "The Great Fire of Madura", we commemorated the War's end.

A few days later we flew the Spitfires to China Bay, a Fleet Air Arm base on Ceylon's east coast, where they were embarked on to HMS *Trumpeter*, the escort-carrier which was to bear us to Malaya. D-Day was September 8th; nine Spitfires from Number 11 Squadron and nine from Number 17 were aboard the carrier. Of the eighteen, one-third were designated potential wastage, perhaps an over-handsome casualty allowance, but the Order of Battle (which we had seen) catered for putting ashore a formation of twelve fighter-reconnaissance aircraft. I contrived a last-minute farewell trip to Colombo in the back of an ancient Swordfish, which was still within the airfield's perimeter five minutes after take-off, battling nobly against a strong headwind as it puffed and snorted on its strenuous headway. One of the left-behind Spits took off and within seconds had hurtled past the poor old Stringbag, whose maximum speed was about ninety.

Trumpeter, our home for the next week, provided every comfort except against what now seemed the crass stupidity of a deck take-off, when the "invasion" could no longer have any possible significance. We hoped that the Japanese in Malaya had heard about their surrender. Examining the anemometer which indicated the speed of the wind over the carrier's deck, we were told that we could not get airborne without a minimum surface wind of five knots which, added to the carrier's flat-out speed of eighteen knots, gave a total of twenty-three knots, the minimum necessary for safe take-off. Each knot was worth five extra feet of deck, and five hundred and fifty feet was supposed to be the minimum to allow a Spit XIV to get airborne. A fifteen feet drop from the deck to the sea was a bit of spare, provided take-off was gauged to allow the aircraft to reach the end of the deck at the moment the carrier was pitching, as opposed to tossing. That was the responsibility of the batsmen, who signalled the pilots to wind up — that is open the throttle and build up engine power against the hold of the brakes, then at the fall of the bat release the brakes and ram the throttle fully open. To give additional lift the ground crews fashioned wooden chocks to be placed betwen the wings and the flaps, first lowered while the chocks were put in place then partially raised, when they remained lowered by twenty-three degrees — about a quarter of their full traverse, but giving maximum lift.

September 8th came and went and no word with it, but next day our habitual siesta was interrupted by the metallic voice of the tannoy ordering all RAF pilots to the ready-room for take-off briefing. There we assembled grumpily in flying-kit to be told that we would be met at our landing-field, Kelanang, some two hundred miles north of Singapore, by the RAF Servicing Commandos, due to have stormed ashore the preceding day, and that the RAF Regiment would be there to guard, house and provision us. On deck the anemometer read eighteen knots — the sea was like glass, with not a breath of necessary surface wind. From the huge lifts emerged the aircraft which had been stowed in the hangars below deck.

"The fools — we'll all be killed!" snarled Captain Bill, "they know we need twenty-three knots to get off!" He had been hitting the bottle hard for some weeks and his nerve had deserted him. Quite suddenly I found myself infected by his fear, frightened as I had never been before. Miserably I crawled into the cockpit of my Spitfire, strapped on my parachute and safety harness, adjusted helmet, goggles and oxygen-mask, and waited to be manhandled into position for the take-off. We started the mighty engines. It was about to happen.

Wing Commander Smith, a calm Canadian, went off first, to disappear off the end of the deck. It seemed a long time before he emerged, water dripping from the blades of his airscrew. He had touched the drink. His Numbers Two and Three staggered off untidily after him, joining into a V-formation, then it was the turn of the next trio, led by Eastman, our acting Squadron Commander. He repeated the Wing Commander's performance. Before he had disappeared over the end I was in position behind him, tense and pale, and the batsmen were winding me up. You can bloody wait till I'm ready, I thought grimly, and took my time, conscious of the tight faces straining at me from the wretched control superstructure on the wrong side of the deck and from the catwalks around its edges. Still no Eastman as I opened the throttle and clamped the brake-lever hard. The great Griffon engine roared, the Spitfire's tail lifted and the wheels started sliding out of the brakes' grasp. All at the same moment I rammed the throttle fully open and released my sweaty grip on the brake-lever, applying full left rudder and aileron, and muttering a silent prayer. The blessed Spit responded like a perfect angel and I was airborne almost before my eyes were opened again.

Hallelujah! and there was Eastman ahead of and below me, staggering up from the ocean which he had hit along the whole length of his plane. The charm had not deserted him. The agonising interval between his take-off and mine could not have been more than five seconds. I lowered my flaps to jettison the wooden chocks then immediately raised them again. Throttling

230

back, I tucked in happily on his starboard side as our Number Three appeared to make up our "Vic", or arrowhead formation, then there was the coast of Malaya, invisible from *Trumpeter*, winding dejectedly ahead under grey cloud, until a few minutes later we were circling Kelanang airstrip prior to landing. It was packed with red-roundelled Japanese warplanes lined up in neat rows, but not a sign of the Wingco's vic of three aircraft who must have landed by now. Eastman and I exchanged uneasy glances but for some obscure reason continued to observe the rule of radio silence. Suspicions of oriental treachery flashed through my mind — the Japs must have carved up the first three as they landed and were waiting gloatingly for us muggins. But we had no option — without deck-landing apparatus we simply had to land there. Down we went, and as I touched down I saw two of the Wingco's vic in crazy postures towards the end of the runway — one up on its nose, the other down on one wing-tip; of the third there was no sign. Obvious treachery! I would gun my Spit from the three-point landing position up to the horizontal and blast the Japs with my cannon in a farewell bout of mutual destruction. As we slowed down a group of Jap airmen appeared and waved us forward; meekly we taxied towards them. Backing away into the surrounding jungle the perimeter track led to a parking apron where the third Spit of the Wingco's Vic stood tidily at rest beneath the trees, its pilot and the other two surrounded by Jap airmen, the lot of them calmly smoking cigarettes, which satisfied me that at least their heads were still on. Obedient to the signals of the Japanese ground crew we parked in line, switched off and climbed out to join the party.

"It's as soft as shit," the Wing Commander said cheerily, "I went up on my nose. These chaps came to the rescue and waved Bill in." So far from treachery, the Japs were actually being helpful. They must have been told of the surrender.

It was an exciting and curious moment — the release from the carrier's confinement, our arrival in a new country with a new smell, and the very odd company in which we found ourselves; real live Japs by the score, looking for all the world like ordinary humans. They were surprisingly plump and well-dressed, well-equipped and obviously well-fed; they looked happy, and displayed quantities of gold teeth at us, all the time bowing, hissing, and saluting politely. I could imagine them serving groceries but not cutting off heads, not seriously anyway. Were these the equivalent of our glossy Headquarters gentlemen?

"Well, where are the Servicing Commandos?" I asked, but they were not to turn up until several days later. Soon all the Spits had landed, the wastage unused, and the question arose of where we were going to lay our heads. Except by the Japs, we were seemingly quite unexpected. It was considerate of our invasion planners to have let them know we were arriving. We trooped off to inspect the airfield, passing rows of wooden huts which housed the enemy airmen, and so to the far end of the field where stood an empty house, which we took over as our quarters. All we had was what we stood up in plus some specially-printed-for-the-invasion Malay money — no sleeping-bags, no change of clothing, no food, no cooking utensils. It was getting late, we were hungry, and there was only one thing for it. Feeling foolish and very fed-up we walked to the Jap camp and ignominiously begged a few biscuits. That was supper.

"We'd better bloody well get out our escape kit and do a bit of fishing before it's dark," someone suggested; but in the manner of tropical countries it was dark before you could say knife. The commandeered house included one cave-like room whose windows and door were of fine mosquito-proof mesh; we herded into it for the first of several uncomfortable nights. Stretched out on bare boards we waited, freezing, for daylight. There was a sense of not being welcome, except to the mosquitoes which laughingly penetrated the screens. At a nearby village next morning we managed to buy eggs, milk and some lamps, then settled down to await the Servicing Commandos and RAF Regiment. The day passed without sight or sound of a manjack of them. Growing tetchy as well as hungry we set off for the landing beaches at Morib, a few miles away and did rather well, coming away with a small truck, laden with neat wooden crates of rations, a couple of primus stoves and hurricane lamps, and the necessary fuel for them all. The beach was the epitome of confusion. Some seventy men had apparently drowned with their vehicles during the unopposed landings, due to a planner's miscalculation of the tides. We saw tank and troop landing-craft and lorries offshore and awash, stuck in the mud. Angry soldiers were demanding petrol for a convoy of lorries laden with troops which had been sent off to the capital, Kuala Lumpur, inadequately fuelled, and which had conked out half way there; stores stacked along a half-mile strip of beach were still being unloaded, while a sweating Beachmaster rushed hither and thither, shouting and brandishing sheaves of documents; cosy little tented camps set up in the dunes at the back of the beach harboured sundry military tea-parties, shaded from the blistering sun. We talked with an officer of the leading assault party of two days earlier.

"A bloody shambles!" he snorted angrily. "Every Nip for miles around, fifty thousand of them, are sitting up there (indicating the high ground dominating the beach) with every bloody gun in Malaya pointing down the beach, and laughing themselves bloody sick. If this had been opposed it would have been bloody slaughter — another Gallipoli!"

Shortly after getting back to the airfield we were visited by the Air Officer Commanding, who rolled up in a splendid amphibious vehicle known as a "Duck".

"How's it going, boys?", he asked.

We told him.

"I'd better get back to my Headquarters ship then," he said sensibly, and went.

Next day our visitor was none other than the Supremo himself.

"The purpose of Operation Zipper," he explained, "has been to show the enemy what they could have expected had they opposed us." It was unbelievable! He could not have been ignorant of the chaos, so we refrained from comment. I noted the hair sprouting generously from his nostrils and ears. He too returned to his Headquarters ship, where I hope he and his staff — all staff, everywhere, always — were more comfortable and less hungry than we in our strange, cold, bare house.

CHAPTER
TWELVE

Urbanisation

The next day, with still no sign of Commandos or Regiment, we set off in our truck for Kuala Lumpur, driving along good tarmac roads girdled by paddyfields. As we passed through villages ornate with triumphal arches and flags, large crowds of Malay Chinese rushed to welcome us, leaping on to the running-board of the truck or running excitedly alongside, clapping and cheering. There was no doubting the intensity of their pleasure or the warmth of their welcome. "So very happy to see you, so glad to see you back," said one, pumping away at my hand while tears streamed down his face. We were the first British servicemen to pass through since the surrender, and received similar acclaim all along our route. A simple wonderment overcame me that our presence could mean so much to those people, and everything that had gone before began to seem worth while; it was a relief. Along the roadside in the open country, groups of peasants stopped and bowed at the truck's approach, until they realised we were British and not Japanese, their moonlike faces split in wide delighted smiles, and they waved and shouted at us, hopping about in beaming joy. Shortly before reaching Kuala Lumpur we were stopped at yet another village, asked by a Chinese to go to his house, as he gravely needed help. In a palatial abode he fed us iced coffee, pineapple and rich cake, and told us about his string of racehorses. Politely we asked what help he could possibly need of us. Solemnly he led us into an adjoining room, where on a couch lay a living skeleton. The creature was barely recognisable as a human being. He was a skeleton stretched over with taut yellow skin and a pair of saucer-like brown pools in the eye sockets. His arms were as thick as his bones, roughly the girth of a man's thumb, with shrunken played-out tennis-balls for elbows. The legs were similar, the head a skull with ears and sere skin, the awful, pitiful eyes, and where his hair should be there was one entire festering scab. The creature tried to smile.

"We got him out of a Jap prison last week," our host told us. "He is sixteen years old. Three years ago he was captured helping the communist guerillas in the hills; he was offered the choice of turning informer or joining the Kempeitai (the Japanese Secret Police) to spy on his own people. He refused both, and this is what they have done to him. You have vitamin pills; can you give some to the boy?"

True, we had vitamin pills in the neat little ration-boxes we had picked up at the beach, and promised to return next day with a supply. We left filled with horror at what we had witnessed.

Next day, after duly delivering a supply of pills, we went on to the capital, where on the airfield the garrison of ten thousand Japanese soldiers had been standing to attention in the boiling sun since early in the morning, participating in the official surrender parade at which they publicly handed over their guns and swords. The idea was to disgrace them — make them lose face with the Malays. The sight amazed us who, until a few days earlier, had never seen more than a handful of the invisible enemy we had been fighting. Kuala Lumpur itself had been taken over by Chinese soldiers in green uniforms, the guerillas who had been harrying the Japanese from the nearby mountains, supplied from the air by the Allies, and who were later to cause inordinate trouble. Their caps were adorned with red stars, and they became known as "the Hennessy boys". Back at the airfield, the guard of twelve Japanese soldiers rose to the salute as we drove in to witness the closing stages of the surrender ceremony. A high wailed order from the Japanese Commander was repeated down the ranks of men, and for a moment I expected a massive shout of "Banzai" followed by a suicidal onslaught in final token of humiliation and despair. Such was the reputation of the Japanese forces. But they were too well-disciplined for that, and a file of diminutive officers one by one unbuckled their long swords and handed them into a lorry, the Commander at the end of the queue. By now the garrison had been standing to attention in the unshaded heat for ten hours. The place reeked of the strange petrol mixture they used in their vehicles, distilled from potatoes or something, a hot, flat pungent smell which embossed itself into the odorific memory. I received a Japanese sword from one of the Army officers in charge of the surrender, to mark our presence on the occasion. Twenty-two years later I was to present it and my Japanese flag to 11 Squadron at the celebration of its fiftieth anniversary.

Back at Kelanang, Mackenzie, a gentle giant who had flown on 11 Squadron for many years, undertook the responsibilities of cook to our small party. His habitual attire consisted of a towel used as a loincloth. Out of the commando rations he contrived all manner of magnificent spread. The rations were "European", the stuff they'd enjoyed in that theatre of war — none of the dehydrated swill we had lived on in the jungle, but tinned stews and soups, real butter, succulent tinned fruits, bacon, creamy condensed milk, salt and pepper, biscuits which were edible, and cake — we feasted like lords. The high humidity rate caused excessive sweating and consequent salt loss, against which we took concentrated salt pills. After one of the cook's splendid puddings, imaginatively devised out of ground edible biscuits mixed with cocoa, condensed milk and sugar, I remembered that I was in arrear with my salt pill intake, and knocked back several. I should have anticipated that they would react emetically, but the cook was frightfully upset, thinking it was his pudding that had done it. He murmured an apology which he was to repeat a couple of months later, on a somewhat different occasion.

A mere six days late, the Servicing Commandos arrived to look after our planes, followed a day later by the RAF Regiment. We went down to the tarmac to see how the Commandos were getting on with the Spits.

239

They weren't getting on too well as they had been trained on Wellington bombers which is what they had been told they were going to service. They had never before seen the Spit XIV, with their quaint high-explosive cartridge-starter device, and had already exhausted the whole supply of cartridges without managing to get a single Spit started. We were well and truly grounded. Happily, the situation was remedied a few days later, and we were airborne to show the flag over a series of surrender parades at sundry regional capitals. Our own ground crews arrived and we moved to Kuala Lumpur airfield, there to sample the fruits of lush living. Visiting the wealthy Chinaman with a fresh supply of vitamin pills for the skeleton boy, we learnt that he had died the day after our last visit.

The RAF organisation quickly found its feet, and struck normal form by sending us to Tengah, a crummy tarmac-runwayed strip on Singapore island, two days after we had arrived at K. L. After another two days it was discovered that where they had really meant to send us was Seletar, a large peacetime station north-east of the town, fronting the Straits of Johore; Seletar was also a flying-boat base, and in the water of the Straits sat a squadron of Sunderlands, as calm as a covey of pregnant ducks. The two Spitfire squadrons and two squadrons of very snazzy Mosquito light bombers were arrayed on the large airfield. The Mosquito was made of wood sections glued together, but which unfortunately tended to come unstuck in the extreme heat and humidity of that Equatorial region. Aerobatics with them were forbidden, but the prohibition was disregarded by one crew, while we watched their display. Then it shed a wing as it approached for its landing, the plane plummeted into the ground before the men inside had a chance to bale out, and the all too familiar column of dense black oil smoke leapt from their pyre. The man standing next to me, a beribboned veteran, burst into tears. It was too much.

Jap prisoners were made to labour a twelve hour day in the full sun, side by side with their Korean comfort-girls, the most unprepossessing of females. Despite the awful atrocities they had perpetrated towards their own captives, including women, I felt sorry for the prisoners. One simply had to harden one's heart. But the business of loving my brothers had caused much misgiving throughout my war career, and somehow I felt that the Almighty had failed to make adequate communication. The Germans and we had both invoked (presumably the same) God to bless our respective banners and ensure that right triumphed, and we had wiped each other out by the million. And did God really approve the extermination of six million Jews, and all those Poles and Russians? What about my West African brothers whose mental age was about eight, and who looked on me as a father? And my uneducated Egyptian brothers whose hostility drove cheek-turning out of mind. The Indians, were they my brothers, their thinking as remote from mine as my own from theirs? The Burmese, who betrayed us at Sinthe? The Japs themselves, should I have loved them as my brothers, yet demonstrate my love by slaughtering them? As for the pity I felt for them now, should I not in the continuing battle for survival beware of the emotion? So far I had not sufficiently experienced frailty in others to inculcate tenderness. "If you find yourselves feeling sorry for the prisoners," advised one of the visiting generals, "go down to the military hospital in the town and take a look at what they've done to our chaps who were in their hands." I left my heart hard, and perhaps the decision was wise.

The hangars at Seletar were littered with abandoned enemy aircraft, including Bakas ("The Fool") — diminutive suicide planes flown by Kamikaze pilots. At Johore, over the causeway connecting the island with the mainland, we browsed curiously over dwarf one-man tanks, abandoned by the roadside. Singapore itself, approached down an expansive avenue designed for speeding, was one of those fascinating, tumultuous cities which vibrated like a dynamo, always a-hum with the intensive industry of its largely Chinese population. There were temples and shrines to gawk at, long narrow streets along which to wander, packed with curio shops each delineated by a projecting banner. Pleasure gardens like enormous fairgrounds offered every worldly delight; there were theatres where brilliantly-clad performers postured in grotesque exaggeration, to the deafening accompaniment of blaring trumpets and the clash of outsize cymbals; stalls rush-lit at night dispensed fragrant dishes of birdsnest soup, bamboo shoots and other delicacies; and always the subtle scent of incense billowed from a multitude of censers and tapers throughout the teeming town. Flowing from hidden drawers, from underneath floorboards, from secret cellars and locked chests, attractive merchandise appeared which had been hidden away from the occupying Japanese, almost specifically designed, it seemed, to satisfy the compulsive needs of men for long deprived of shops and the ability to spend accumulated earnings. Like magpies we seized the glittering cameras and wristwatches, bargaining cigarettes and clothing not available to the civilians and which in consequence commanded large values. The Chinese, natural and sophisticated merchants against whom the indigenous Malays were sweet innocent babes, constituted three-fourths of the population, and their commercial methods seemed pleasantly uncomplicated in contrast with the subtlety of the Egyptians and Indians. We stocked not only what satisfied our immediate requirements, but the gifts which in due course we would take home. With alarm I discovered that on their maps the Japanese coloured their country and empire red, placing their islands in a central position, privileges which were surely British? Did they really not know that was our colour, and that their proper place was over on the far right?

With ten-cent dancing-girls in pyjama suits or long-slit robes clinging tightly to their slimness, we carried out the socially acceptable fornication-suggestion of the blue-lit ballroom — the licensed sex-substitute, vertical licentiousness — never lacking hope that the inuendo might lead to a major horizontal

243

engagement, yet at the same time accepting the minor fulfilment of simple physical contact. But before long, tiring of the phoney convention (and, in my case, surprisingly undaunted by or forgetful of the experiences of Alexandria and Calcutta) we discovered an acceptable bordello staffed by admirable Chinese girls, skilful at putting one at one's ease and thereby rendering the transaction relaxed.

Trumpeter arrived in the mighty harbour, and in the launch on the way out to the reunion celebrations, threading among the great fleet of junks tethered in the placid waters, I was seasick. Several of the airmen, drinking in low clubs, became seriously ill through wood-alcohol brews deadly to the optic nerve; three of them lost their sight, one permanently.

My twenty-fifth birthday eased by casually, and the fairground seer had miscalculated the odds. Excitingly, the town filled up with Dutch ladies evacuated from the East Indian islands, but they were carefully cloistered in chaste camps to which they had to return by ten each evening. An invitation which we issued to a Christmas party to be held in the Seletar Mess was vetoed by their Commandant, a stern, plump lady in her middle years, whose hair was dyed. In desperation we sent an imprecatory delegation, which by including her in the invitation as most-honoured guest, persuaded a change of mind. The dance which we arranged started off as a first-class flop; it was soon evident that the Commandant's rigid presence was putting a gigantic damper on the proceedings. Conferences between groups of officers led to my being loaded with the responsibility of syphoning her off. Suitable quantities of the Station's rum ration, allied doubtless with her deprivations through the years of incarceration, stimulated the casting-off of her inhibitions, and unsteadily she and I withdrew, leaving the floor clear for the others. Some time later the gentle giant, Mackenzie, chose to come into my room to borrow a comb, switched on the light, and was suitably confused at discovering the Commandant and me in a compromising situation. Once again he blurted out his apologetic phrase as he beat a swift retreat, switching off the light as he went. When the Commandant and I got back to the ballroom I was accorded a hero's ovation; the party had ended up a success. "I am ze Commandant," the lady insisted, although nobody was contesting the point, and her statement could be heard disappearing faintly into the brilliant tropical night as the entertainment broke up and the guests departed. When I called next day to pay my respects she not only bore no animosity but seemed keen on a repeat performance.

That same room, which I shared with Eddie Carlton, my "oppo", now possessor of the Distinguished Flying Cross, was the scene of a recurring event involving the Chinese servant we shared. Ming Hong Koon, who resembled a great, anxious, yellow balloon, was pallid through the excesses of the opium smoking which had him in his grip. Each morning at seven Eddie awoke with a thundering hangover to yell for poor Ming, whose sandalled feet pattered down the stone corridor. At the sight of the jaundiced face illuminating the doorway, Eddie shouted angrily for tea, and off Ming pattered to return a few minutes later bearing the steaming beverage. Bad-temperedly Eddie grunted, as he thrust a shaking hand under his mosquito-net and, quaking from his own excesses, Ming Hong Koon rattled the teacup in its saucer until Eddie's quavering hand and Ming's trembling saucer arrived in adequate juxtaposition for the desired transfer. There followed a nerve-wracking interval before their shakes became synchronised and the cup could change hands. The tea was downed with a single gulp, and red in the face Eddie was asleep again before the Chinaman had departed. Poor oppo. A few weeks later the charm deserted him, and he too died an airman's death as a harmless little Auster span him into eternity, to become part of his own song.

Down on the airfield, Ginger Lacey, a Battle of Britain ace who commanded Number 17 Squadron executed a beat-up so magnificently low that his airscrew touched the ground, but the charm held and all that he lost was twelve inches of each of the five blades. Another pilot was saved from mangling by the armour plate behind the seat of his Spit when the airscrew of a second Spitfire, landing too close behind him, minced his plane to shreds from tail to cockpit while I watched helpless from a thousand feet above them, unable to yell a warning when I saw what was going to happen because my radio was defective. Comforts arrived from suddenly-generous institutions at home, in the form of thermos flasks, penknives, and similarly useless baubles, but starved of personal possessions we cherished the trinkets.

"What did you get, Ginger?" the Station Commander enquired of 17 Squadron's CO; they were standing at the bar.

"This, Sir," and Ginger pulled out a shiny new penknife.

"Is it sharp?" The Group Captain asked ingenuously.

"I think so, Sir," and as he replied Ginger opened one of the blades and cut off the Groupie's tie, just below the knot. A hush descended, as the Group Captain looked down at the forlorn pieces of black tie at his feet. Then, "You shit, Ginger!" he yelled, and red in the face and with eyes a-squint made for the slender Squadron Leader, who adroitly beat a hasty retreat into the night, hotly pursued by a vengeful Station Commander, roaring threats of awful vengeance.

In January 1946, as we were preparing to leave for Japan as part of the occupation force, I was offered repatriation. I had no desire for it — there was nothing for which to return. The flow of letters I had maintained through thick and thin had increasingly become addressed to shadows. The only real thing in my life had become the sharing of hardship with comrades, an impermeable sense of exile, and a deep love of and need for flying. Of course I was off-balance, still jungle-happy, perhaps even still sand-happy. I had survived only through a kind of emotional castration. My entire adult life had been spent preparing for, learning and then enduring the agonies, dangers and delights of flying and destroying, integrated within intimate groups of brave young men, voluntarily electing for manly living. I was used to courage and strength, decisiveness and generosity, qualities I admired as much as I despised cowardice, weakness and pettiness. Pity had not been inculcated in us. I did not relish becoming a Headquarters wallah in England. My dead Oppo and I had worked out a scheme for a modest air service between Singapore, Bangkok, Saigon and Batavia, flying de Havilland Rapides; had we followed it through, it would undoubtedly have succeeded. We knew nothing but flying, we wanted nothing else. But he died. And now I was being invited home.

A letter from home told of family illness; I resolved my mental and spiritual tussle, deciding to accept repatriation in the full knowledge that it marked the end of the first, and possibly most important, phase in my adult life. I arranged matters so that at dawn on the same morning as the Spitfires were to take off for Japan I would have left Seletar ahead of them in one of the Sunderlands. The preceding night witnessed a drunken farewell party in the Mess, when the traditional games of indoor rugby and hi-cockalorum — a version of the Eton wall game — were played with customary vigour and dash, and the usual casualties were carried off to bed or hospital, according to the severity of their injuries. I was presented with an elaborate document subscribed to by the pilots, testifying to my mental stability, physical well-being, and suitability for employment in an appropriately menial position in civilian life. Our current CO, a diminutive Scot known as the Wee MacGregor, insisted on a final round of his favourite game, where side by side at the bar two players took alternate smites at the nearer biceps muscle of the other, until one cried mercy and bought the victor a drink. I was at least half as heavy again as the Wee One and resisted his invitaion to the unequal joust, but he was adamant, tears running down his cheeks, because it was my last night on the Squadron. Obligingly I hammered him into speedy submission.

It was announced that the Sunderland flight to Madras had been postponed twenty-four hours, and I sank into swift despair. I would now be left behind by the departing Squadron instead of leaving it, exactly what I had schemed to avoid. The party broke up at dawn, when two of the pilots went down to their planes for a whiff of oxygen, a palliative for hangovers. That early morning it was more than a palliative, as two Spitfires roared over the Mess, slow-rolling drunkenly at fifty feet and arousing the whole Station. That they managed to avoid killing themselves was perplexing, explicable only in terms of the magic charm in their lives continuing. Later that morning, one by one the Squadron flew off for Japan, as I stood beside the runway waving to each in turn. Sick at heart I wandered despondently back to the Mess and up to my room, along the empty corridor to the deserted quarters. Aimless and dejected I span out the day, the longest and most miserable I have ever known, for I had time to realise that a long-accustomed way of life had been ruptured, and that what lay ahead held no attraction. Uncarroted, a blue tomorrow stretched before me, laden with clouds of uncertainty and doubt. Hesitation, misgiving, regret and insecurity embalmed me suffocatingly; misery overcame me.

CHAPTER
THIRTEEN

A Troopship Leaving Bombay

The huge flying-boat rocked gently in the waters of the Johore Straits, skittishly dipping a sponson into the supporting ripples which glistened in the first light of the steamy tropical day. I had not slept, but had lain listening to the bullfrogs' infernal mating racket until the three-thirty call, an hour before dawn take-off. I looked forward to leaving the elements of earth and water and to accepting the joyous relish of the air, to which the years had conditioned me. In successive crescendos the white Sunderland's engines drew the stepped hull free of the clinging water into the peace of the sky, and I relaxed while the crew settled down to the chores of the fifteen hundred mile non-stop journey to Madras. Allowed to take over from George, the automatic pilot, I found the boat as unwieldy as a London Transport bus after the delicate responsiveness of the Spitfire. For just under twelve hours the Sunderland chundered along like some old grannie of the heavens, before descending into the dazzling sea where it licks benignly at red Madras.

I spent the next thirty-six hours in a train across the subcontinent to Bombay, my travelling companion a silent Indian gentleman whose bearer trotted up the corridor from time to time laden with foods, the odour of which became intolerable in that confinement and inculcated what was to become a lifetime abhorrence of Indian cuisine. Those of us without servants obtained nutrition from station restaurants during the long stops provided for the purpose, the heavy carriages pausing in their stroll across the teeming brown face of that vivid country. Worli, outside Bombay, was a dull, functional camp filled with airmen awaiting embarkation for home after their years abroad. With few exceptions, of whom I was one, they were older men returning to be demobilised; they contributed to the morose atmosphere of the place, for they were old enough to have been married before the war and now looked positively sick at the prospect of returning to their procrastinated anxieties and responsibilities, hardly improved by prolonged absences from home and especially separation from their wives. Their boat was due to sail at the end of the week.

Next day the list was posted of those who would be on the following boat, three weeks later, and as my name was not included I knew I was in for a stimulating month or two at Worli — the sort of hanging around which is part of RAF life. Bombay was reputed to be a lively place, with plenty to see and do. I would spend my first week sorting out my possessions and ideas, make a cosy list or two, and avoid becoming surfeited with the town — experience had by now taught me that ten days of any place is more than enough for the traveller who cannot become assimilated.

During that week I lay soaking in the sun on a last session of scorching worship. On my fifth evening I was required to report to the Orderly Room. For once I hadn't done anything, so it surely couldn't be that I was in trouble for some unknown transgression. Be ready, I was told, to leave at six tomorrow morning, for embarkation at seven! But why? Because four men out of the fifteen hundred already stowed aboard Capetown Castle for the morrow's departure had been put ashore, sick, their places were being filled by repatriates, as distinct from demobees, and I was one of the few available. By two o'clock next morning the myriad bits of necessary paper had been completed and signed, and my belongings sorted, packed and marked. Sleep was out of the question, my mind racing wildly in disbelief at what had long seemed an impossibility — I was returning home, the agonised dream of nearly four long years suddenly transmuted into truth. When Johnny comes marching home, marching home, marching home . . . My head span dizzily.

At six on a hot clear morning the four of us piled our baggage onto a truck and climbed familiarly over the tailboard, to bump down to the quay beside the Gateway of India, a noble monument outside the Taj Mahal Hotel. With scant ceremony the gangplank of the large troopship *Capetown Castle* was heaved up almost before we were aboard, the captain obviously concerned about tides. The throng at the ship's landward rail was uproarious as an Indian band temerously played *Will Ye No' Come Back Again*. The hawsers were cast off and the large ship slid silently away. I found myself alongside a tall, attractive W A A F officer, dabbing at startlingly blue eyes in between waving a damp handkerchief in the direction of a uniformed gentleman below on the dockside. Here after all was the troopship just leaving Bombay about which we had sung so hilariously, so furiously and so eternally, in those arid, hopeless camps around the world. I passed a dry handkerchief to the damsel, who took it without even noticing her lean, brown, wolflike and obviously kindly neighbour.

I shared a cabin with three other officers returning for demobilisation, one of whom was George Lansworth, a poet, who had also been long away from England and warned that the Socialists would be waiting for us when we got back and that would be that for the lot of us. More he would not divulge, but the future became heavy with foreboding as *Capetown Castle* sidled through the Suez Canal, passing the El Firdan airfield which had been my home two and a half years earlier. From the Port Said dhows I acquired some of the homecoming gifts denied through my unexpected departure from Worli. "Lend me your ear," demanded Lansworth, anxious for appreciation of his iambic pentameters, "does this scan?" Temporarily more concerned with love than poetry I escaped as soon as courtesy permitted. As we passed Pantelleria a few days later the sun retired gracefully from my life, and the uncertain temperate climate assumed its domination. Rolling across the Bay of Biscay nobody looked sicker than the Indian and Anglo-Indian brides brought home by some of the airmen; unused to the damp, cold European winter they muffled unavailingly in ill-cut coats; just as the passage of time had bleached the West African ladies, so their darkness became revealed in the brides to whom their brilliant tropical sun was more flattering than the grey northern atmosphere. As we pulled alongside the quay at Southampton Lansworth growled finally, "There they are, the Socialists, waiting for us," and on that cold, wet, grey January day of 1946, against the unromantic background of Southampton Docks, the ashen faces peering unsmilingly up seemed to explain his sinister prognostications. One of the faces, surmounting an RAF uniform, came aboard and confronted me, insisting that he was my young brother. So changed a person was I, so changed in appearance was he, being by then twenty-one, that even after he had identified himself I failed to recognise one who had always been very close to me. The shock was the first of many which were to bring my head down from the open skies, away from the colourful rows of campaign medals, away from the cherished wings with their red silk fighter-boy's crown, away from the camaraderie of war, down to a painfully drawn-out acceptance of brutal reality.

As the troop-train pulled away for London and the North, Lansworth was still on the quayside by the railway lines, capstans and giant chains, arguing the toss with a Customs officer to whom he had failed to disclose the contents of an enormous crateful of Indian carpets. I never understood how he had hoped to sneak it through. Non-stop through London the train raced its human cargo, which pressed a thousand noses against grimy panes to take in the stark, wintry landscape, somehow unbelievably beautiful and utterly unfamiliar. At Liverpool more grey ones accepted us with the grim attitude we were soon to recognise, and even though I was promptly despatched on indefinite leave, the prison-propensities of England in the early months of 1946 became increasingly apparent. I felt a total prisoner, though I had only been deprived of freedom of horizon. The tiny red dots on the map which through the years of exile had steadily diminished in size, significance and influence, now assumed a cheerless domination as the immutable establishment, untouched by the years of war, relentlessly crushed our newly captive spirits. Only the beauty of the countryside relieved the grimness of post-war Britain.

At Fighter Command Headquarters I was offered the unhappy choice between signing on for one year's flying or accepting a ground job pending demobilisation about three months later. Unavailingly I pleaded for a five-year flying commission, as it was obvious to even the most unbusinesslike fighter-pilot that a one-year contract would simply put a man that length of time behind the rest entering civilian life. The multi-engined bus drivers were being signed up by airlines, but the split-arse fighter-pilot might make the passengers airsick. During two months at West Malling in Kent, my dreary routine as a flying-controller was remitted by visits to the Norfolk-based blue-eyed WAAF officer, in a maroon pre-war Austin Seven bought with my enforced savings; and by a trip in a Spitfire IX when I frightened the life out of myself, lost in impenetrable mist from the moment of becoming airborne until, eighty-five minutes later and with a thimbleful of petrol left, I found myself back over the airfield, my charm still hard at work, to make a perfect three-point landing. I knew I had flown my last.

It fell to my lot to command a Station Parade. I had scant idea of what it was all about, but turned up punctually at the parade ground. The Station Warrant Officer marched smartly from the parading thousands towards me, stopped with a crash, saluted muscularly, and when I responded politely muttered, "If you don't know what to do, Sir, just face the parade and leave it to me." He had obviously come across my type before. Gratefully I accepted the suggestion, and as he marched back to his ordained pitch I shambled to the front of the assembled multitude. They gazed at me blankly while I stood waiting and wondering. It was like suddenly being pushed from the wings into the middle of the floodlit stage of a packed theatre. The SWO was true to his promise, crashing towards me, stamping noisily and saluting again. I knew what to do about that. I returned his salute. He crashed around to face the mob.

"Pa-rade!" he bawled, "At-ten . . . tion! Stand at . . . ease! At-ten . . . tion!" and they did, the whole lot of them did exactly that. So did I, realising too late that being in charge, so to speak, I should not have responded to those uncontradictable commands. The

SWO had his back to me and didn't see. He executed a crisp right-about-turn, came close up to me briskly, stamped and saluted once more, so did I, though I was beginning to get that feeling of losing my balance. He took three purposeful steps backwards, ending up with another resounding stamp and still facing me. I looked intently into his granite eyes, awaiting a sign.

"Parade — stand at ease," he mouthed at me, not a muscle moving in his resolute face, and so that nobody else heard a sound. Dutifully I repeated the phrase in my most stentorian voice, in which any fool could detect the apprehension. Yet astonishingly as one man the parade stood at ease. The SWO had established a mood of compliance which even I could not upset.

"Parade — atten-tion," came the next hiss, beautifully controlled; I was more or less lip-reading, my adrenal gland working overtime. They stamped to Attention.

"Parade — for inspection — open order — march!" It was beginning to come back, all that square-bashing we had done on the promenade at Skegness, and on the parade ground at Leuchars with that wax-moustachioed bastard, all those lifetimes ago, and I bet it had been going on all the time we were in the East bashing hell out of the Huns and Nips. I warmed to the business, we had a thoroughly good parade, and everyone went home satisfied, even the SWO, though I bet on returning to the NCOs' Mess he told them of the typical half-trained type of officer who doesn't know his left foot from his right, I don't know what the bloody Air Force is coming to these days.

May 1946 saw my return to my parents' home, aged twenty-five, hair prematurely thinning, but complete with demobilisation suit, shirt, hat and shoes, and £400 in the bank, money I'd been unable to spend in Burma plus a handsome gratuity of nearly thirty bob for each month's War service to set me up in life. I wondered how much the men who'd stayed behind had rung up, and thought, as I so often did, of all the young men who had died. An indulgent beat-up in London suitably reduced my fortune as I turned to face the future.

CHAPTER
FOURTEEN

Aftermath

Any fine day in the ensuing ten years turned my eyes and heart towards the skies, and the sound of aero-engines has never ceased to be music. Yet I retain two recurrent nightmares. In the first I am airborne low over a road, and above my head run tramway-wires from which there is no escape except by contrived awakening — shades of the Crewe balloon barrage. In the other I am an onlooker at some crazy young pilot carrying out reckless aerobatics too close to the ground, and I know that he will eventually crash and burn up. I yell inaudible warnings to save his sweet youthful life, but inevitably the charm deserts him and he hits the ground a short distance away. I rush towards him weeping, knowing the machine will burst into flames before I can reach him. The familiar black column erupts and climbs over him as I race to drag him from the blazing wreck, even though he is always hanging scorched in his harness, dead. Sometimes in anguished frenzy I manage to pull him free, and for a moment his body jerks nervously to life in my hands before collapsing in a stiff agony of blackened extinction. And I think that it is myself that I am watching.

Where are they now, the souls of my dead comrades? The bodies of my colourful still-living friends? Skegness Sergeant, are you one of the cheerful battered faces I see on television tending the needs of the young men boxing their way to fame and fortune? Slim little blonde, are you ferrying your grandchildren in prams along the roads of a housing estate grown over the airfields from which you flew your Spitfires and Halifaxes? My pathetic Takoradi comedian, did you make the grade, and is your life now satisfactorily obsessed with some pioneer theatre? Bubbling Michelle, are you grown old and fat like the rest of us and, tired of your sagging remains, is Leon discreetly unfaithful to you? You, Bill Fender, must have become a successful dynamic relentless tycoon, your life a web of money and the material comforts it buys; and you, Cairns, surely a top adman. Mowbray, I have no doubt, is a whisky salesman with a strawberry nose, boring the locals from one end of the evening bar; and Molly Malone — soul of sweet kindliness — how lucky those of us whose lives you have touched. Are the bullfrogs still honking in the mysterious Chettinad pool, or is it now part of a vast desolate swamp? Headquarters wallahs everywhere, entrench yourselves still deeper in the index-linked corridors of power, awaiting the honours and pensions which are your due. You, Ginger, I know remained an airman for many years, doubtless cutting off ever more senior officers' ties. Young men whose lives the charm did not desert, are you now bald and white and aching like me? Did your lives too become harassed and anxious, looking back in sad

261

pleasure and forward in harrowing uncertainty, concerned in caring, wrapped in triviality, hopeful still while optimism wanes, unconfident that honour is immortal, perplexed at soft enthusiasms, grim at insipid arrogance? Dead men, spared our hesitancies, are your souls at rest?

About the blue-eyed WAAF officer I know pretty well everything that one human being can know of another, and she of me, for almost a year to the day after our meeting we married.

Tropics

Names that excite me —
Lagos, Lavinia,
Flames that overpower me,
Suns that devour me,
Shores that delight me
Beyond contemplation.

Hues that impel me —
Magenta, indigo,
Blues of the Middle Sea,
Vermilion to befuddle me,
Shades that overwhelm me
With rich suffocation.

Beaches of burnished sands —
Matruh, Ratmalana,
Palm-leaves that embrace me,
Smooth balms that ease me,
Lush fruits from slender hands
For thirst's saturation.

Eastward my heart returns —
Melir, Misurata,
There where the temples stand
Quivering in distant lands,

Where mind and body spurn
Life's termination.

Soul of the glowing sphere —
Libya, Malaya,
Passion that cries out to me,
Ecstasy to shout to me
Recall! Remember
The wild animation!

Warmth of the summer tide —
Blue the wide heavens,
Brown skin that tormented me,
Hotly contented me,
Trembled my savage bride,
Sun of temptation.

Flowers in glistening hair —
Jasmine, bougainvillea,
Perfumes that incense me,
Breath that must convince me,
Languid the heavy air
Wreathing elation.

Worlds that elude me —
Burma and Lebanon:
Futile fingers chide me,
Vanished wraiths deride me,
Tropics that delude me
Pass to oblivion.

Also available in ISIS Large Print:

My Life as a Spy

Leslie Woodhead

In the spring of 1956, 18-year-old Leslie Woodhead received a summons to serve Her Majesty. National Service signalled the end of boyhood. But it was the beginning of his "life as a spy".

An only child, living above a shop in post-war Halifax, Woodhead grew up with austerity and secrets. But nothing prepared him for the comically bleak RAF training camps he now found himself in, nor the isolated Joint Services School for Linguistics on the East coast of Scotland. Here he was trained by a colourful staff of émigrés, who taught a course of total immersion in Russian for purposes not always clear to their pupils. A posting to an ex-Luftwaffe base in a war-scarred Berlin provided only partial explanations. In the ruins of a city gripped by espionage and paranoia, he discovers adulthood and his vocation as an observer and documenter of people.

ISBN 0-7531-9366-3 (hb)
ISBN 0-7531-9367-1 (pb)

A Somerset Airman

Eric Gardner

At the age of 19, Eric Gardner joined the RAF. His witty observations of day-to-day life as an airman in wartime Britain and Canada give a fascinating insight into the life experienced by many ordinary men and women, from all backgrounds, who were brought together by World War Two.

Like many of his generation, Eric did not receive a higher education and was unable to fulfil his obvious potential. In later life, he often commented that the RAF had been his university.

Eric thought his wartime experiences would be of little interest to anyone else because he did not see any active service. His family thankfully did not agree and encouraged him to commit his memories to paper. He finished the manuscript just days before his sudden death at the age of 82 and so, sadly, Eric never saw it in print.

ISBN 0-7531-9352-3 **(hb)**
ISBN 0-7531-9353-1 **(pb)**

Friends and Romans

John Miller

With a single daring leap from an Italian train carrying prisoners of war, John Miller jumped out of the war of soldiers and into the war as lived by Italian civilians . . . many of whom risked their lives to help him.

The year was 1943 and Captain Miller had been in captivity for over a year. Italian anti-fascists harboured and fed him, first in a remote mountain village, then in Rome itself. For months he posed as a deaf-mute and member of the Fascist Youth in order to dodge German patrols and the Italian secret police . . . until the Allied liberation of Rome brought GIs flooding onto the streets.

This is a war memoir with a difference, in which the heroics are those of ordinary people and everyday life, in which a fugitive forms an intimate bond with people from another culture . . . and comes to realise the ironies of national conflict.

ISBN 0-7531-9342-6 **(hb)**
ISBN 0-7531-9343-4 **(pb)**

They Also Serve

Dorothy Baden-Powell

At the Scandinavian Section of the SOE, Dorothy Baden-Powell was engaged in sending saboteurs into occupied Norway and debriefing them on their return to London. After spending a year and a half with the SOE, she was given an assignment in the WRNS to try to break a ring of enemy spies. They were based on HMS Raleigh, a naval training camp at Plymouth and were sending information to Germany about the movements of British warships from nearly every port in the United Kingdom. She endured the privations of life on the lower deck, the unwelcome scrutiny of a particularly unpleasant WRNS Superintendent, and a trumped-up charge and subsequent court-martial.

Finally, she uncovered an enemy agent trying to be taken on as a sailor, and by a combination of bravery, sheer determination and luck, succeeded in having him captured. With her assignment successfully completed she gladly returned to her job with the SOE.

ISBN 0-7531-9336-1 (hb)
ISBN 0-7531-9337-X (pb)